What people are saying about...

Discovering Celtic Christianity

"*Discovering Celtic Christianity* is a must read for anyone interested in learning more about and experiencing the wisdom of the Celtic saints. It takes the reader on a pilgrimage, a spiritual journey through the Celtic religious sites in Great Britain and Ireland. Remembering the pilgrims who have gone before us, like the Celtic saints, can inspire and draw us closer to God. The story of one of my favorite spiritual guides, Brigit of Kildarem shows the rich treasury of faith and spirituality her memory continues to stir in contemporary seekers. Reading this book has led me to reflect more deeply on my own wonderful Celtic heritage. It also makes me want to make a sacred journey to some of these beautiful sites."

Bridget Mary Meehan
Author, *Praying with Women of the Bible*

"Dr. Pullen's reflections in the context of his travel journal reveal the difficulty of maintaining the ancient attitude of pilgrimage in a contemporary culture. Yet through the obvious intensity of his travels he sees through the hurry with what the Celtic Christians called 'the eye of the eagle.' His historical observations are illuminating. Better still, his reflections on the relevance of the values of Celtic Christianity once again underscore a significant point: The current popularity of Celtic Christianity is no mere Celtic nostalgia, but the seeking of a more whole, more encompassing path of discipleship in grievously fragmented times."

The Rev. Jack Stapleton
St. Aidan Celtic Christian Trust, USA

"Dr. Pullen has done a good job of providing a very accessible and readable history of Celtic Christianity. Other histories exist, of course, but tend to be far more scholarly and not aimed at the general reading public. The short entries from Dr. Pullen's personal diary interweave a touch of warmth into the historical narrative. The pilgrim theme is a rich and inviting one. Dr. Pullen effectively cradles the narrative in journal entries from his own pilgrimage. This technique makes what could otherwise be a mere historical narrative into something very human and contemporary. By including the sections inviting personal reflection along with prayers and scriptural references, he emulates the finest of Celtic tradition which combines the search for learning with the quest for God."

John J. Young, Ph.D.
Dean, Division of Continual Learning of N.C.

"Bruce Pullen's *Discovering Celtic Christianity* is a highly informative exposition of Celtic spirituality and its relevance for today. Part history, part journal, it also contains helpful questions for both personal reflections and group discussions. Designed for today's pilgrims, its overall contents (including bibliography, historical charts, and a list of bed-and-breakfasts and small hotels) make it a useful guide for those desirous of exploring the holy sites of the Celtic saints."

Edward Sellner
Professor of Theology and Spirituality
College of St. Catherine
St. Paul, Minnesota
Author, *Wisdom of the Celtic Saints*

Discovering
CELTIC
CHRISTIANITY

Its Roots, Relationships, and Relevance

Bruce Reed Pullen

To Tom

God's Blessings on your journeys
Good to travel with you in Ireland
Bruce R Pullen

XXIII

TWENTY-THIRD PUBLICATIONS
Mystic, CT 06355

Christian now went to the spring, and drank thereof, to refresh himself, and then began to go up the hill, saying:

> The hill, though high, I covet to ascend,
> The difficulty will not me offend;
> For I perceive the way to life lies here.
> Come, pluck up heart, let us neither faint nor fear;
> Better, though difficult, the right way to go,
> Than wrong, though easy, where the end is woe.

The Pilgrim's Progress
John Bunyan, 1678

Twenty-Third Publications
185 Willow Street
P.O. Box 180
Mystic, CT 06355
(860) 536-2611
(800) 321-0411

ISBN: 0-89622-927-0
Library of Congress Catalog Card Number: 98-60275
Printed in the U.S.A.

DEDICATION

ACKNOWLEDGMENTS

Pilgrims Who Walked with Me

My special thanks to my congregation in Westfield, Massachusetts for graciously granting me a study leave and the denomination I serve for giving me a grant to help with the cost of my studies. Special thanks to my wife, Judith Ann Pullen; my administrative assistant, Harriet Stewart; and the other members of the two pilot study groups that met with me to share their tales of ways taken and not taken. The recommendations of pilgrims Diane Shearer, JoAnn Tombeck, and Carole Woods whom I met during my study leave and who read my first draft are deeply appreciated. The encouraging words in letter and in person by Celtic author Esther de Waal, made this journey memorable.

I discovered Celtic Christianity only recently, so I am deeply indebted to those who have written in the area of Celtic studies. The books that have influenced me are listed in the selected bibliography. I have tried to credit everyone whose work I have quoted. The stories of the Celtic saints and sites have been passed down orally and in written form for hundreds of years. They have been retold here from my particular point of view.

CONTENTS

PART THREE - RELEVANCE

Celtic Quest

A Quest for Meaning

Welcome to this brief introduction to Celtic Christianity. Many books are available that discuss particular aspects of Celtic Christianity (some are listed at the close of this book in Guidebooks for the Pilgrim—A Selected Bibliography). There are, however, very few general introductions to the personalities, places, and problems associated with the development of Celtic Christianity. That is what this book offers.

My own personal Celtic quest began with the question, "How did the Christian faith first come to Great Britain?" The answer may surprise you as it did me for, although Christianity originally arrived in Britain with the invasion of the Roman army, the Celts later reintroduced a form of Christianity that was different from the Christianity in practice on the continent. I felt challenged to read more about the Celts and then to visit the sites where these saints lived their lives next to God, so one summer I undertook a pilgrimage to Great Britain and Ireland.

This book is my pilgrimage, the soul friends I met, and the thin places I visited. True pilgrimage transforms, and my life has been influenced by that journey. It will never be the same. Join me now on a Celtic Quest. You will learn something about Celtic Christianity in the process; perhaps you will also learn something about yourself.

We are all born in the middle of what is happening around us. We join our families, friends, and acquaintances; we walk with them for a while; and then we also drop out of the journey. Between birth and death we seek to make some sense of our lives. The act of seeking something is a quest, a search. In our quest for meaning and purpose we often find an answer in the vision that flows from the faith journeys of others. The saints of Celtic Christianity sought to make sense of the pieces of their lives, their hearts, souls, and minds—as do we.

On the journey of the soul, the spiritual part of our journey, we either move toward or away from a loving God. We respond to God's love by loving God and loving people. As we do, we may move from being pagans or agnostics (those who have little or no faith in God) to believers (those who do). The journey does not end there. The next step along the path toward spiritual maturity is discipleship. We join a Christian community to learn more about how we may find peace with God. The final step is becoming an apostle. In the early church this meant being a missionary. We become missionaries when we share the faith we hold with someone else. We pass on to others what we believe and understand, what makes sense of the pieces of our lives, in the hope that they will also enjoy the promise of a full life. Thus, the faith is passed from generation to generation.

The Roots of our Faith

Faith is often born and then nurtured within the same community. This has been so for me. The church in which my parents were members formed a congregation of caring people who nurtured my faith and eventually ordained me. It will always be my home church, a place filled with fond memories, a place where I have roots. That congregation's family tree has its roots in Great Britain where our particular branch of the Christian faith first took shape and grew. When I first traveled to Britain, I focused on the architecture of more than thirty cathedrals from Durham to Coventry, York to Canterbury, Ely to Salisbury. These magnificent houses of worship, built to the "glory of God," remain an inspiring part of our Christian heritage.

During the first millennium Christianity spread through Britain and Ireland in a variety of ways, but one way—some would argue the major or most influential way—was shaped by the Celts, pronounced Kelts, or Keltoi as the Greeks called them (Latin gives it a soft "c" as in the "Boston Celtics"). The Celtic Christians enthusiastically shared their faith with others. Their way eventually clashed with the ever-expanding influence of the Roman church. At the Synod of Whitby in 664 the king adopted the Roman order and the Celtic way soon became the "way not taken." That way faded from the world scene, but its influence continues.

A Spiritual Journey

My Celtic Quest inspired me to plan a spiritual journey to Great Britain and Ireland to visit saints and sites that are part of the Celtic heritage. Two Celtic traditions, "soul friends" and "thin places," shaped both my pilgrimage and the format of this book. An Anamchara or "soul friend" is a spiritual advisor. According to Celtic tradition, this person is a mentor or guiding spirit who helps us discover how God is calling us to a better, more meaningful life. "Thin places" are sites where we may experience a very thin line between heaven and earth.

One summer, then, I became a pilgrim, journeying to many of these thin places, sites where Celtic Christianity took root, flourished, and spread through Scotland, Wales, Ireland, and Northern England. On the Pullen shield there are three scallop shells, symbolizing pilgrimage. That sign originated in Spain where tradition says James, one of the twelve, was a missionary who, upon returning to Jerusalem, was beheaded by Herod Agrippa. The myth then arose that his remains were transported to Compostela. A shrine was built there in hopes that pilgrims would come. Come they did! Compostela became the most visited city in the West during the Middle Ages. And when the pilgrims left, they took with them a scallop shell as a souvenir of their journey (gladly sold to them by enterprising Compostela fishermen). The scallop shell soon became the badge of the pilgrim, appearing on statues of James, on stained glass windows, on family crests, and as a sign, worn round the neck. Who my pilgrim ancestor is I will probably never know, but as a modern day pilgrim, I claim the sign of pilgrimage.

Pilgrimage is still a leaving of our normal routine, a launching out on a journey, and a returning home, transformed. Like pilgrims before us, we are searching. Two things matter: first, deciding where to go, then discovering something about ourselves along the way. Pilgrimage, with its time to reflect, is as crucial today as it ever was.

Summary

Part One will introduce the concept of pilgrimage, then the people we call Celts, and finally the Romans who occupied Britain bringing with them the first wave of the Christian faith.

Part Two briefly introduces the saints and their sites, reflects on an aspect of Celtic Christianity, and concludes with a brief meditation. Our journey begins with Ninian and Whithorn, the cradle of Celtic Christianity, and moves chronologically to Hilda and Whitby where the Celtic form of Christianity clashed with the Roman, becoming "the way not taken."

Part Three summarizes the characteristics of the Celtic way and suggests ways in which the Celtic model may be resurfacing.

This book is written in chronological order according to the history, places, and events of the Celtic people. My own pilgrimage, however, did not always follow the same time line. Thus, the entries from my journal, here titled Pilgrim Travels, will not always appear in order of occurrence.

The new millennium will usher in new challenges for we are once again surrounded by a pagan society. Celtic Christianity, developed by those who lived in a pagan era, made disciples in a pagan world. Discover now a way of life that flourished for a while and then faded from view to be reborn, I believe, in a new millennium. As you search for meaning and purpose in your own life, may your quest be a Celtic one. And may our journey together make a difference in your life.

Bruce Reed Pullen
Westfield, Massachusetts
May 1998

The hill, though high, I covet to ascend,
The difficulty will not me offend...

Am I an Old World animal?
A creature of peaty grass and rain?
A cast-off Celt longing for home?
How else to explain this curious alienation from
my New World life, my longing to dig my boots
in heather and tough bracken and remain.

Diane J. Shearer[1]

PART ONE

Celtic Roots

The ultimate pilgrimage is the spiritual journey we all experience from birth through life to death. How we make that journey reflects our understanding of God and the world in which we live. We may choose to move toward God or to move in another direction. The success of the twelve-step program, initially with alcoholics and now with a wide variety of addictions, lies in its basic invitation to choose life, a life lived along a path that seeks the help of a Higher Power, whom some call God. The pilgrim way toward God brings life, peace, and wholeness; the other, death, destruction, and disease.

If you believe that you are born, live, die, and that's it, the focus of your pilgrimage might be that you are remembered by "the personal relationships you have experienced, the creations you have left behind, the communities in which you have lived, and the joy and sorrow to which you have given birth."[2] This may seem to be enough for some. For persons of faith, however, the focus of our pilgrimage is a deep and abiding friendship with the God we worship and wish to be with forever. The road for the Christian pilgrim is the way modeled by Jesus of Nazareth.

In Chapter One you are invited to explore the world of the pilgrim and then to join us on a Celtic Quest, a pilgrimage through these pages of the saints and sites of Celtic Christianity. We begin with what it means to be a pilgrim, continue with some reflections on pilgrim travel and what it means to be a pilgrim today, and conclude by joining the psalmist as he contemplates returning home from his pilgrimage to Jerusalem. Each chapter concludes with a prayer in the Celtic style.

In Chapter Two we learn more about the Celtic people, their life-style and their religion. The Celts were a unique, pagan people who were probably shaped and molded as a culture in what is now Switzerland and Austria. Branches of Celtic culture settled in Britain and Ireland and in Galatia where Paul wrote to them. Their faith in an afterlife paved the way for a ready acceptance of the Christian faith when it arrived on their shores.

And arrive it did with the Roman invasion of Britain. Chapter Three tells of the Roman occupation of Britain which lasted more than 350 years. The Romans imported their own unique life-style and culture to this distant land. With them—unofficially—came the Christian faith.

As I wrote in the opening section, Celtic Quest, our journey to spiritual maturity takes us from being pagans to believers to disciples to apostles. Although we are all on the same journey, not all of us are at the same place on the path. Some are pagans searching for faith in something or someone beyond them. Others have found faith in God, but see that as an ending rather than a beginning. Disciples seek to learn more about the faith they hold. The last stage of spiritual maturity is sharing the good news with others.

In the Middle Ages Geoffrey Chaucer wrote The Canterbury Tales, a unique work based on the concept of pilgrims drawn from all walks of life making their journey to Canterbury, and making that journey more enjoyable by telling tales about their lives. In Tales We Tell Along the Way in the epilogue there are some suggestions for group study based on the ·Scripture text found in each chapter. You are invited to gather in small groups to share your tale with other pilgrims. Read the chapter, reflect on the related Scripture text, and share your tales with those who walk with you on your pilgrim journey.

May your pilgrimage inspire you to return home from your explorations with a better understanding of who you are in relation to God and the people who love you.

Time Line: Part One

Dates are often uncertain. c=circa, around that time

3000-2500 BC	Passage graves at Newgrange and Knowth (c.2500); Stonehenge begun.
2700	Beaker (distinctive pottery) people begin arriving in Britain.
2400	The Bronze Age begins, followed by the Iron Age (700-300).
750-450	La Tene, Switzerland - Celtic culture is identified.
c. 300-600	The Celts gradually emigrate to Britain.
c. 500-350	Celts begin arriving in Ireland.
387	Celts sack Rome.
280	Celts descend into Macedonia (Galatia).
64-52	Caesar invades Gaul and makes foray into Britain, 55 BC.
30-33 AD	Jesus comes to proclaim the good news.
43	The Romans begin the conquest of Britain; Scotland is invaded in 83.
50+	Paul's letters. Paul writes to the Galatians in 55.
60+	Gospels are compiled; Mark is probably the first.
70	Destruction of Jerusalem by Titus.
122	Hadrian visits Britain and orders a wall built across Britain in the north in 123.
180	Early signs of Christianity in Britain at Chedworth.
313	Edict of Milan. Christianity becomes a favored religion under Constantine who had served in York, Britain and returned to Rome to become emperor.

Canterbury

*Slane —
Ruins*

*Knowth —
Burial Mound*

Hadrian's Wall

1

The Pilgrim

I look to the hills! Where will I find help?
It will come from the Lord,
who created the heavens and the earth. . . .
The Lord will protect you now and always wherever you go.

Psalm 121

PILGRIM TRAVELS

Monday, July 1

The first wave of the Christian faith hit the shores of Britain with the Roman army. Almost four hundred years later when the Romans left, the flame of faith was kept burning by small pockets of Celtic Christians. Robert Van de Weyer, in the closing chapter of *Celtic Fire*, suggests places to visit where the Celtic saints trod and lived close to God. Inspired, I make plans to visit some of these sites. The critical first step is deciding where and when to go. Help comes from my rapidly expanding Celtic library, several Celtic conferences, and a Celtic newsletter, *Anamchairde*. Now a visit seems a must! So on Monday, July 1, I find myself driving to the airport to begin what will be a renewing and life-changing experience.

Pilgrimage

People gather for worship for many reasons but certainly one is to continue their spiritual journey toward God with others. They come as pilgrims on a quest in search of the holy.

When someone mentions "pilgrimage," what comes to mind? At first you may recall Abraham, the father of our faith, and his pilgrimage to connect with the "one God" rather than worshiping the many gods of his people. Or you may think of Chaucer's pilgrims on the road to Canterbury Cathedral. You may picture the Mayflower and the Pilgrims who sailed to New England to practice their faith in freedom. Finally, the image that comes to mind may be of a contemporary pilgrimage, a search for the holy among the smorgasbord of choices offered by various religious groups today.

A "pilgrim" is one who dedicates a period of time to the search for the holy, for a closer experience of the living God. The pilgrim travels light and wears comfortable clothing. Serious pilgrims combine both the outward journey toward a holy place and the inward journey toward self-understanding. Humor and laughter help to make the journey enjoyable when both frustrations and fun, rain and rainbows, and stark scenery and beautiful horizons are encountered along the way. Worship, both private and public, is often part of the journey. A pilgrim is patient, knowing that eventually the journey will end in arrival, and in that arriving will be blessings as never before.

Marks of the Pilgrim

This image, both positive and powerful, reveals seven characteristics of the pilgrim.

1. Quest: searching for what is ultimately important, moving toward a goal.

2. Flexibility: adapting to the situation, for there are many paths to our destination.

3. Patience: calmly enduring trying situations.

4. Simplicity: taking only what we need with us.

5. Dedication: committing ourselves to achieving the goal.

6. Risk: taking a chance that what lies ahead is better than what has been.

7. Joy: delighting in what we encounter along the way.

We all have had brief pilgrimages, short, renewing periods of movement in which we attempt to refocus the journey, to renew our lives, to rekindle the fire within us. Such moments of movement in search of meaning alternate with periods of remaining in place. Such is the balance we have and need in our lives. We move and regroup. We pick up our tents and wander and then, finding a good campsite, we pitch them, remaining for a while before moving on again. To that extent we are all pilgrims on a pilgrimage.

What Is a Pilgrimage?

1. *Pilgrimage is purposeful; it has a destination.* The goal may be to return to a place full of memories, a place where you experienced a range of emotions from joy to sadness. Perhaps it is a place where you grew up, or went to school, or served in the armed forces. Often it is a place where you bonded with others. Many things will have changed, not the least yourself, often making the returning a bittersweet experience.

Recently a friend, born in Poland in the thirties, revisited the places of his childhood with his daughter, who was living in Poland. He was one of the fortunate survivors of the Nazi holocaust that imprisoned and killed thousands of Polish children. It was a deeply moving experience for both father and daughter. Perhaps you can recall such an event in your own life.

2. *Pilgrimage is renewing.* You may be drawn to a place although you don't know why or what you are seeking there. You just have a feeling that this is where you should be. When we wander from the way, we sense the need to draw closer to God. A pilgrimage may put us back on track by reminding us of lessons learned and forgotten, of places whose beauty we had overlooked, and of friends and loved ones we had taken for granted.

Little Gidding, the site of a former religious community near Cambridge, was founded in the seventeenth century by Nicholas Ferrar. In 1936, T. S. Eliot, the St. Louis-born poet, visited the site and wrote of the experience in "Little Gidding," which is included in *Four Quartets*. The Friends of Little Gidding was formed and they restored the original chapel. Sarah and Robert Van de Weyer created a new Christian community there. On the way to Wales I stopped overnight at the center and chatted with Robert about my pilgrimage. I enjoyed evening worship with the community, which uses a prayer book they have compiled to worship together each day.

3. *Pilgrimage is a time for reflection.* The saints sometimes spent hours in prayerful reflection. We have an opportunity during a pilgrimage to reflect on what has happened thus far in our lives and to create a vision of where we would like to go.

At the beginning of his ministry Jesus took time to retreat into the desert wilderness to reflect on his mission. These days of contemplation helped him focus his ministry for the years ahead. During those years Jesus repeatedly withdrew to reflect before moving on with the work of the day. In the evening he would spend time again in prayer before facing a new day.

4. *When pilgrimage includes other pilgrims, the excitement of the journey is shared.* Under the leadership of Moses the people of God gathered regularly to renew their covenant. This renewal service became a festival, a time of pilgrimage to the sanctuary where the ark rested. Eventually the pilgrimage was transferred to the temple in Jerusalem. After the exile, the people of faith dreamed of renewing the pilgrim journey to Jerusalem. The songs sung by these postexilic pilgrims on their way to and from Jerusalem are found in Psalms 120 to 134. Luke records Jesus and his family taking such a pilgrim journey to Jerusalem for the Passover (2:41).

5. *Pilgrimage transforms us.* Pilgrimage is not a trip or a tour. Pilgrimage is an inward as well as an outward journey. Along the way we gain new insights on how to live and also a better appreciation of those with whom we live.

Pilgrimage is visiting a place that has been made holy by what has occurred there in the past, worshiping there with other pilgrims, and then leaving the site with transformed lives. Remember that pilgrims can be in many different places on their spiritual journey. Some may just be starting, some will be walking with us, and others will be way ahead of us. What matters is that we are moving in the right direction.

Brigid, the spiritual advisor for a generation of Irish, counsels us that we all need a guide or "soul friend" on our journey to help us reflect on where we are going. Ciaran tells us that certain places, "thin places," enable us to feel closer to God.

Have you ever had moments when you felt closer to God? Have you ever told someone else about that experience? Chances are you have not; virtually no one does because most people feel embarrassed talking about their faith. Sharing those moments with a friend is important. When you witness to others about how important your faith is in your life, as did the Celtic saints, you help them to believe that what they are turning toward, life forever with God, is better than what they are leaving behind, and that the journey is worth the risk.

Closing Reflection: Pilgrimage Today

Travel that fulfills some sort of spiritual quest is definitely on the rise. Millions are making brief pilgrimages every year in an attempt to draw closer to their God. Thousands of pilgrims flock to the Celtic Christian religious sites in Great Britain and Ireland each summer, sites such as Iona in Scotland, St. Davids in Wales, Lindisfarne or Holy Island in northern England, and Clonmacnoise and Glendalough in Ireland. A few may even reach Skellig Michael, the island off the coast of Ireland that contains the little-changed remains of a religious community. Few of the original buildings remain at these sites since most were constructed of wood, but even the stones that endure inspire since we know they were touched by lives lived close to God.

Coventry Cathedral: A Place of Pilgrimage

Coventry Cathedral in England, destroyed by bombing during World War II, is today a place of pilgrimage. Within the ruins stands a wooden cross created out of the burned wood from the original structure and a cross shaped from the original hand-crafted nails. A beautiful, modern cathedral stands next to it on which is a stunning image of Michael, the archangel, subduing the fallen Lucifer. Entering the sanctuary, you spy a huge tapestry of the risen Christ. As you turn to leave, you view the ruins beyond through the angels incised in the clear glass windows. A special film presentation calls modern pilgrims to work at a ministry of peace and reconciliation. The "cross of nails" pin is a symbol of that mission. Pilgrimage here is a memorable, often life-changing, experience.

The Roads We Take

Life has its deadlines; the final one is death. That fact challenges us to make the most of the time we have. The closer to the end we come, the more we are confronted by the final accounting of who we are, what we have been, and the roads we have taken.

Alfred Nobel, the inventor of dynamite, awoke one morning to find his obituary in the paper. He would be remembered, the newspaper indicated, for his invention of the greatest destructive force of his day. Confronted by that accounting, Nobel decided to create a force for peace, the Nobel Peace Prize.

Robert Frost in his classic poem, "The Road Not Taken," indicates that there are points along the way when the road divides, and we have to choose which one we will take.

Choices do make a difference. Although we cannot change the past, we have the gift of the present in which to move toward a life-style that leads to "Shalom" wholeness, the integration of the emotional, spiritual, and intellectual, so that we might truly love God "with all our heart, soul, and mind," and love other people as we love ourselves.

How then shall we live given the parameters of birth and death? When the road divides, which path shall we take? We invite you to take the way that leads to God, the way not taken by so many. The roads we take do make a difference. Love God. Love people. Share your faith.

Faith Sharing: A Pilgrim's Psalm

I lift up my eyes to the hills—
from where will my help come?
My help comes from the Lord,
who made heaven and earth.
He will not let your foot be moved;
he who keeps you will not slumber.
He who keeps Israel
will neither slumber nor sleep.

The Lord is your keeper;
the Lord is your shade at your right hand.
The sun shall not strike you by day,
nor the moon by night.
The Lord will keep you from all evil;
he will keep your life.
The Lord will keep your going out and your coming in
from this time on and forevermore.

Psalm 121

Called "songs of ascents," Psalms 120-134 were sung as pilgrims climbed the hills to Jerusalem. Psalm 121 is often interpreted as a dialogue between a pilgrim and a priest, a farewell liturgy, the priest closing with a blessing. The pilgrim has made the journey, possibly at Passover, possibly with other pilgrims, to worship in Jerusalem. Although anxious over the return journey, the pilgrim knows the source that will provide help along the way. With faith renewed and God's blessing, the pilgrim leaves the sacred place for the journey home.

Personal Reflection

1. Perhaps the toughest choices we make are made each day when the road forks and we must choose the way. Reflect on where you get your support and guidance for those choices.

2. We all make brief pilgrimages in our lives in which we attempt to refocus our journey, to renew our lives, to rekindle the fire. Recall a pilgrimage you made. Did it transform your life?

Closing Prayer

As we walk this day with God, our Creator;
As we walk this day with Jesus, our Savior;
As we walk this day with the Spirit, our Guide;
We walk with the Trinity and the Trinity
walks with us as we journey along life's way.
Bless, O God, our pilgrimage path. Amen.

2
The Celts

Leave your country, your family, and your relatives
and go to the land that I will show you.
I will bless you and make your descendants into a great nation.
You will become famous and be a blessing to others.

Genesis 12:1–2

PILGRIM TRAVELS

Wednesday, July 3
The Isle of Mull, Scotland

The Oban ferry lands at the tiny village of Craignure and the crowds move quickly to the tour buses. The buses wind their way thirty-seven miles along a single-lane road lined with turnouts for passing. Along the way to the Iona ferry at Fionnphort I spy some spectacular mountain scenery including the moorlands that rise up to Ben More, Mull's highest peak (3,169 feet). Icy mountain streams, some of which supply water to the homes below, dot the landscape.

A *crannog*, a man-made island in the middle of a small lake, comes into view. A circular timber-framed thatched house up to thirty feet in diameter would have been built on it. The Celts created such islands by sinking boulders and driving wooden piles into the water bed ("cran" is Irish for a tree). The water barrier protected the family and their herds from predators both wild and human.

It is more than forty-eight hours since I left home. Nearing my first major goal, Iona, I am tired and traveling light, running on nervous energy and immersed in the experience. The hope grows that in this journey I will be blessed. It is beginning to feel like a pilgrimage.

Tuesday, July 16
Newgrange and Knowth, Ireland

Two weeks later and I am in Ireland. After the Ice Age receded, people began arriving in Ireland where they constructed megalithic monuments known as passage graves, circular mounds with a central burial chamber entered by a stone-lined passageway. One of the reasons why Christianity spread in Ireland with so little resistance is the already held belief in an afterlife indicated by these passage graves. There are three passage graves in the Boyne Valley: Knowth, Dowth, and Newgrange. Newgrange's brilliant white quartz front is now restored and an entrance has been added into the burial chamber. The central mound at Knowth, built c. 2500 BC, is forty feet high by two hundred twenty feet in diameter and houses the largest collection of neolithic art in Europe. Beautiful, complex, abstract designs are carved into its stone retaining walls. Workers are constructing an entrance to make these treasures more accessible for future pilgrims.

Saturday, July 20
Navan Fort, Northern Ireland

Navan Fort, once one of the most important places in Ulster, lies just outside of Armagh. An architecturally award-winning educational center nestles in a mound of earth. Its outstanding audiovisual presentation of the old Celtic tales associated with Emain Macha, the legendary capital of Ulster, combines sight and sound, reminiscent of *Riverdance*, creating an enthralling narrative. The actual fort, a mile hike from the center, is deserted now.

The People Called Celts

The Celts developed a culture so distinctive from other European races that its nuances are felt even now. Often, when differing cultures agree to live together, languages and traditions merge to form a new culture. The Urnfield people, whose ancestors came from the east where the Ur-people lived, and the Scythians merged during the period of 750-450 BC to form the unique people we call the Celts. Evidence of their culture was found in Hallstatt in Upper Austria and later at La Tene, a tiny village in Switzerland. By 300 BC they had branched out from there into northern Italy, Britain, Ireland, Spain, and France.

The Celts wrote little about themselves so what we know comes from archaeological research and their enemies' somewhat prejudiced descriptions. Julius Caesar wrote, "Gaul consists of three distinct regions, inhabited respectively by the Belgae, the Aquitani, and a people who call themselves Celts, but are known to us as Galli."[1]

Migration into Italy

Around 400 BC, a large number of Celts migrated across the Alps and seized the fertile Po valley. From there they spread out over northern Italy where they enjoyed a simple life of fighting and farming. Clearing the land with iron axes, they planted rye, wheat, barley for beer, and beans. Grain was stored in pits lined with wicker or stone and sealed with clay. Stone walls surrounded fields which were sized so that they could be plowed in one day with the help of oxen. For meat they raised pigs, cattle, and sheep, and they hunted, using horses, dogs, spears, and steel-tipped arrows.

The Warrior Celts

For centuries, these roving warriors struggled against, and traded with, the Greeks and the Romans. The Celts were tall with fair skin and often thick red hair and blue eyes. Those of high rank often grew moustaches, but otherwise they were clean shaven. Celtic clothes were practical rather than fashionable. The men wore long woolen trousers or *bracae*, and a sleeveless shirt fastened with brooches. The women dressed in brightly colored, long-skirted dresses with a shawl or cloak when it was colder. Materials were patterned with squares and stripes and bright colors predominated, which were obtained from vegetable dyes.

The combat style of the Celts terrified their enemies. Some wore bronze helmets often with horns on them into battle and others covered themselves with breast-armor made out of chains; most of them, both men and women, went naked into battle. They introduced the chariot as a war weapon. They attacked with an uncontrolled fury, cutting off the heads of their enemies and nailing them over their doors as trophies. The ritualized psychological warfare of the Celts, praising their own prowess and insulting their opponents, is still practiced today in pubs.

In 387 BC the Celts marched on Rome, defeating the Roman army near the Tiber River and plundering the city. Then they laid siege to the capitol area where the Romans had retreated. A commando raid late at night was thwarted by the sacred geese, who woke the sleeping Roman sentries with their cackling. After seven months, the Celts negotiated a settlement and withdrew.

Considered barbarians by the classical world, these warlike people nevertheless were carriers of a unique culture which is gradually being rediscovered—a culture whose enduring effect may be discerned in our own day.

The Celts in the New Testament

Three Celtic tribes descended into Macedonia with their families and wagons in the middle of the winter of 280 BC, looting and seeking to settle. Eventually they landed in Galatia, the area of present-day Ankara, Turkey. Their era of dominance ended when an attempted advance on Pergamon was rebuffed in 230 BC. To celebrate the victory, statues of dying Celts were erected in the temple of Athena. Finally in 166 BC the Galatians were decisively defeated and eventually incorporated into the Roman empire.

Gerhard Herm writes in *The Celts* of emotions stirred in him by seeing the famous marble statue of the dying Gaul/Celt in the Capitoline Museum in Rome. "I was touched as I have seldom been by a work of art. The face looking down on me was not at all the 'noble countenance' one reads about but, on the contrary, a face so ordinary that its wearer would not have stood out if he had walked our own streets: unkempt hair, low forehead, slightly snub-nosed, and a Celtic moustache of the type that has for some time been back in fashion. The mouth is half-open and the features are frozen in an expression less of pain than of painful bewilderment…. It was my most direct and personal encounter with a Celt. As I left the museum, I saw hundreds of young men like him sauntering through the streets…young vagabonds from all corners of the earth with blond manes and moustaches…and I said to myself, they are still among us."[2]

Around 55 AD Paul wrote to the Galatians declaring the principles that would define Christianity as a world religion instead of a Jewish sect. He praised them for starting out well, but warned that they now seemed to be falling into their old habits of worshiping idols and getting drunk. He advised them not to boast or challenge others (tough advice for a Celt). His letter pleaded to a people accustomed to putting their trust in the sword, to trust God.

The Celts Come to Britain

Before the Celts arrived in Britain there were the Beaker people and before them the people of the Stone Age. The Beaker people, so called because of their distinctive pottery, began arriving in Britain around 4,700 years ago bringing with them the roots of the English language.

Stonehenge predates the arrival of the Celts. It was built of enormous stones in southern England in stages over a period of 1,500 years beginning 5,000 years ago. One theory states that a small select class of priests, trained in the techniques of predicting the seasons for their farming communities, created religious centers like Stonehenge to both predict and celebrate the changing seasons, including worshiping the sun. Because of its accuracy in predicting movements in the heavens, Gerald Hawkins, an astronomer, writing in *Stonehenge Decoded,* calls it "a neolithic computer," a true astronomical observatory.

Around 2,700 years ago the Celts began arriving in Britain, bringing with them two forms of their language: the Gaelic which survives in Ireland and Scotland; and the Brythonic which was spoken in England and survives in Wales. They also brought their knowledge of smelting bronze and iron, their love of gold, and their weapons of war, giving them an advantage in settling the area. By 100 BC the Celtic life-style and customs were well established in Britain.

The Celts in Wales (Cymru)

Wales is one of the oldest countries in the world. Human life there stretches back more than 200,000 years. Celts began to arrive there from Europe around 600 BC. Celtic kingdoms arose which eventually united in 844. Wales was an independent, prosperous medieval kingdom, producing a great wealth of literature in its Celtic language until the English assumed control in 1415 and eventually annexed it. Although still a part of Great Britain, it remains a Celtic country, proud of its Celtic heritage. Signs are written both in English and Welsh although only a small percentage of the people speak Welsh.

There is a Welsh language television station. The warmth, eloquence, and imagination of the Welsh are a heritage of their Celtic ancestors.

The small island of Mona, also called Ynys Mon or Anglesey, on the northwest coast of Wales was a holy place for Celtic religious life. The Druids were their religious leaders and also the keepers of the law, history, and oral literature of the Celtic civilization.

The Celts in Ireland

Ireland is the only existing Celtic nation-state. The art of Ireland—the illuminated manuscripts and carved stone crosses—is distinctly derived from Celtic art. Celtic culture influenced the early mission of the Christian faith in Ireland, and eventually in Britain.

Although it is difficult to determine when the Celts began arriving in Ireland from central Europe, some believe it was around 500 BC. Rather than congregating in towns, their tendency to be self-reliant resulted in small settlements of circular homesteads. Celtic Ireland at one point was divided into approximately 150 little kingdoms each with its own king. Over time five provinces were formed with a high king elected to rule from Tara. Tara lies near Navan in the gently rolling hills of County Meath. Early Irish tales describe it as the home of heroic gods and goddesses. Lug, the greatest of the Celtic gods, had the power to legitimize the authority of the king. By the ninth century the title "king of Tara" was recognized as that of the most powerful king in Ireland.

Although divided politically, the kingdoms were united by a common language and culture. In the early Celtic period, poets occupied a leading position in Irish society. They acquired their skills in special schools under the direction of the Druids. Since any written language was rudimentary, they memorized their texts and traditions. The great cycles of heroic Celtic sagas originated during this period. These pagan prose epics drew a thin line between life and death, between this world and Tir na nogs, the Land of the Ever Young.

As the number of Celts grew, some settled in hilltop villages (which were easy to defend). There is evidence in Ireland that as early as 300 BC the Celtic tribes ran hospitals caring for the old, the poor, and the sick. Celtic families often included three generations: a husband and wife, along with any single siblings of either, the couple's children, and the couple's parents. Women were respected. They headed extended families, ruled in some noble families, and owned and inherited property. The family worked the farm, everyone helping. As in most primitive societies, some families had slaves that helped with the work. The man who was to become known as St. Patrick was once one of these slaves.

Pre-Christian Celtic Religion

The ties that bound the Celts were language, religion, and law. If, however, you look for a religion common to all the Celts, you will look in vain, for the characteristic feature of Celtic religion is its local nature. Although there are similarities, every region and tribe appears to have had its own particular gods and goddesses. These were gathered in trinities, often portrayed by a three-faced god. Faith was tied to nature and was practiced between the woods and sacred groves. Trees were regarded as divine symbols. In Gaul the oak was venerated; in Britain the yew; and in Ireland the rowan. The Celtic word for oak is "Dhu" as is found in Druid, the word for the Celtic priest. Rivers and springs were often associated with Celtic goddesses.

Their religious life was administered by a well-respected priesthood of Druids who trained from twelve to twenty years, learning their lore by heart. They celebrated four great feasts each year: Imbolg, Beltane, Lughnasad, and Samhain. On November 1 the Celtic year began with Samhain which marked the end of the summer season. October 31 was New Year's Eve, a day when the wall between the natural and supernatural was considered especially thin. The transition from the old to the new year was marked by extinguishing all the fires in Ireland and then relighting them. The Christian faith rebaptized this celebration by calling it All Saints Day, and the previous day All Hallows Eve or Hallowe'en. The other seasons fell every quarter on the first of the month. Imbolog or spring on February 1 became the festival of Brigid. Beltane on May 1 announced the beginning of summer. Lughnasad on August 1 was the harvest festival at which time games and races were held at such royal assembly places as Tara.

The Celts sometimes cremated their dead, often burying them with offerings of food and jewelry. After death, they believed they joined their ancestors in a beautiful place, free from toil and trouble. Happy were those who were invited there.

The Druids also had other functions. They acted as interpreters and judges administering the legal system. The elaborate legislative code was based on community and extended family life. As historians, genealogists, and poets, they memorized and transmitted the history of the clan. These poets were both admired and feared: admired for their learning of folklore and feared for their sarcastic wit which could be used to ridicule one's exploits.

Closing Reflection: Celtic Influence Today

Iona survived the Viking raids and was rebuilt by the Benedictines. Today a few year-round residents remain on the island. The abbey is being refurbished and maintained. The pilgrim experiences the feeling of a thin place here through the religious community which still exists here and continues to work and worship in the Celtic tradition. Iona keeps alive the memory of the ministry and mission that was so important to the bringing of the faith to northern Britain. The ministry of the Iona community and the writings of David Adam at Lindisfarne reflect the revival of the Celtic influence in prayers and worship.

Celtic design illuminates the Lindisfarne Gospels and the Book of Kells. It can still be found in the work of such diverse artists as Archibald Knox from the Isle of Man who, from 1899 to 1912, designed silver and pewter candlesticks, and the Benedictine monks at Christ in the Desert, Abaca, New Mexico who are bringing the tradition of illuminated manuscripts to the Internet.

The great bardic tradition of Celtic poets that sprang from a people carrying their history in oral rather than written form remains in writers such as James Joyce, William Butler Yeats and Seamus Heaney. The songs of Turlough O'Carolan (1670-1738), a blind poet and harpist, have been preserved and are being revived. He is credited by some with creating the tune for "The Star-Spangled Banner."

Examples of Celtic place-names include Cornwall from Cornovii, Devon from Dumnonii, Cumbria from Cymry, and Kent from Cantii. The rivers Tyne, Tees, and Thames are Celtic names.

Celtic influence survives to this day. The Irish, Scots, Welsh, Manx from the Isle of Man, Cornish from Cornwall, and Bretons from Brittany continue to guard the Celtic traditions and language of the people who, in the dawn of history, dominated Europe.

Faith Sharing: The Lord Chooses Abram

Now the Lord said to Abram, "Go from your country and your kindred and your father's house to the land that I will show you. I will make of you a great nation, and I will bless you, and make your name great, so that you will be a blessing. I will bless those who bless you, and the one who curses you I will curse; and in you all the families of the earth shall be blessed."

So Abram went, as the Lord had told him; and Lot went with him. Abram was seventy-five years old when he departed from Haran. Abram took his wife Sarai and his brother's son Lot, and all the possessions that they had gathered, and the persons whom they had acquired in Haran; and they set forth to go to the land of Canaan. When they had come to the land of Canaan, Abram passed through the land to the place at Shechem, to the oak of Moreh. At that time the Canaanites were in the land. Then the Lord appeared to Abram, and said, "To your offspring I will give this land." So he built there an altar to the Lord, who had appeared to him. From there he moved on to the hill country on the east of Bethel, and pitched his tent, with Bethel on the west and Ai on the east; and there he built an altar to the Lord and invoked the name of the Lord. (Genesis 12:1–8)

Abraham (known as Abram before he left on his journey to a new land), is the symbolic father of all Jews, Moslems, and Christians. He was challenged by God to leave home, to travel to an unknown land, and to there begin an entirely new life. So Abraham the pilgrim obeys the call of God. He starts out for his unknown destination traveling one step at a time by faith. All he has is the promise of God that he will be blessed.

God asks us to make a choice as well. God calls us to leave behind the gods of security, tradition, money, time, sex, and success and worship only one God. We may choose to stay or take the first step on the pilgrim journey that will draw us closer to God. The decision to follow God's way often requires sacrifice, so we may be reluctant to begin the journey. But God calls! Will you respond with words something like this? "All right, God, I hear you. I don't know what the journey will bring, but I am going to take the first step." That is the step of faith and God promises to be with us as we take the second and third steps, and all the rest of the steps of the journey until we are home.

The first step in becoming a believer is to pray, "I know you love me, God; help me love you." The next step is to say, "I want to be a disciple and learn more about your way for my life." This may be hard to say; it is even harder to do. Finally, Jesus asks you to invite someone to walk along with you. You probably know several people who are unchurched, that is, who do not regularly go to church. Invite one or all of them to join the journey with you, if not in church, perhaps in the study of this book in your home.

Personal Reflection

1. Our religious heritage changes with each generation. What traditions are important ways of expressing your faith? List them.

2. Are you part of a worshiping community? If not, try exploring a new relationship with God through the means of a community.

Closing Prayer

Come Lord. Come down.
Come in. Come among us.
Come as the wind to move us.
Come as the light to prove us.
Come as the night to rest us.
Come as the storm to test us.
Come as the sun to warm us.
Come as the stillness to calm us.
Come Lord. Come down.
Come in. Come among us.[3]

3

The Romans

I am eager to visit all of you in Rome.

Romans 1:15

PILGRIM TRAVELS

Wednesday, August 14
Chester

The Roman army left behind countless reminders of their occupation—roads, city names, buildings, language. Chester, originally the Roman Fort Deva on the River Dee, is still encircled by a well-preserved, two-mile long, red sandstone city wall. The magnificent cathedral, with its parapets and flying buttresses, is also built of red sandstone. Chester's Roman street pattern, four roads fanning out from the center of the town to the four gates, is still intact. Chester is a delightful city to visit. "The Rows," the ancient (c. 1200), two-level shopping area, is unique.

In the evening, friends and I walked the city wall. I had polio as a child; stairs without handrails are extremely difficult for me. During my first visit to Chester twelve years before, as I struggled to negotiate a set of stairs on the wall sans handrails, two young, husky men, after asking me if I would appreciate help, placed my arms around their shoulders and promptly whisked me down one set of stairs and up another until I was once again on a level path. We all get by with a little help from our friends and the kindness of strangers.

As we walk the wall this time with handrails now in place, we view the Roman Gardens, a collection of Roman stonework from the area. A Confederate flag is flying in one of the apartments nearby, evidence of an invasion of a different sort. Where the wall runs along the River Dee we spy the piers from an old Roman bridge.

Walking the wall at the end of the day this way is a moment in time to be cherished. We came from Massachusetts, Iowa, Michigan, and Missouri for a reunion of sorts. Together we tour the sites, walk the walls, enjoy the meals, take pictures, and buy gifts for home.

A tour with friends, however, is usually not a pilgrimage because the goals are different. A pilgrimage involves introspection and reflection while a tour often focuses on experiencing and enjoying the history and culture of a particular part of a country. For the few guided Celtic pilgrimages available, check the listings quarterly in the *Anamchairde* newsletter.

Hadrian's Wall and Chesters (Cilernum)

Hadrian's Wall is another example of the Roman occupation. It is named for the Roman emperor (117-138) who in 122, while visiting Britain, ordered the building of a great wall to mark the outer northern boundary of the British province. By 130 when the first period of construction was completed, the system consisted of a seventy-three-mile stone wall with sixteen forts, two small forts between each major fort, two turrets between them, and a deep V ditch in front of the wall. It remained the northern frontier during Roman occupation.

A visit to the well-preserved remains at Chesters (not to be confused with Chester above), of a fort that housed a 500-man cavalry unit gave me an overview of what Roman army life was like. The foundations of the fort's headquarters, the chapel, and an officer's house including its attached bathhouse and hypocaust all proclaim the Roman life-style. Three gateways allow for an easy exit for the cavalry. The wall is impressive, not only because it is a unique monument to Roman occupation, but also because some of Britain's most spectacular scenery surrounds it.

Roman Britain

Late in the summer of 43 AD, the Roman army, some 40,000 strong, landed somewhere on the coast of Kent, beginning the invasion of Britain. When the British forces were defeated, the Romans rested until Emperor Claudius could arrive to accept the surrender and the pledge of loyalty of the tribal kings, an important step in the process because Rome depended not only on its army but also its loyal tribal kingdoms to maintain peace in the provinces. The Roman army in Britain consisted of three or four legions with five to six thousand men in each, mostly infantry. It went about gradually placing the country under control. Operating out of their new fortress at Chester, Wales was eventually contained. The Romans then ventured into Caledonia or Scotland where they defeated the Picts. Overextended, they eventually retreated to Britain.

If all of Britain was not conquered, at least it was at peace. In fact, this peace, *Pax Romana*, reigned over the whole known world. The Roman eagle flew unchallenged everywhere. For the first time, it was possible to travel extensively in Britain on the more than 5,000 miles of skillfully engineered roads the Romans created to join the major population centers and military camps. Eventually eight major arteries converged on central Londinium (London) and three major army fortresses were built: Eboracum at York controlling the north, Deva at Chester, and Isca Silurum at Caerleon, Wales occupying the west.

Until recently it was believed that the Roman army never reached Ireland. Irish officials have now confirmed that as early as 79 a Roman coastal fort was located in the village of Drumanagh, 15 miles north of Dublin. Roman coins have been found at some sites.

With the Roman army came new ways of living which were readily adopted by those Celts who did business with them. The Romans soon organized large population centers or cities, in contrast to the Celtic Britons who preferred small communities or villages. The names of Roman cities often include "chester" or "cester," the Roman word for camp. An example would be Worcester or Leicester. The more wealthy and urban Britons soon adopted Roman dress and customs. Some even served in the army, eventually becoming Roman citizens.

Since Latin was the official language, these Britons learned it. Schools were established for educating young Britons, training them in all phases of Roman life. Religion and education were intertwined in the classical world since religious stories laid the foundation for both morals and ethics much as they do today. As temples were erected, the Roman and Celtic gods merged.

Christianity Comes to Britain

The Roman army had developed a worldwide system of roads that radiated out from Rome, facilitating the rapid movement of armies and of information. The church spread rapidly over them since the good news could be carried by evangelists, travelers, and Roman soldiers. Paul could realistically plan to travel over them to Rome and then on to Spain. Without this system it is hard to imagine how long it would have taken for Christianity to spread.

But spread it did. Christian soldiers in the army, Christian merchants and administrators, and other Christians who were attracted to this new province brought the faith with them. Evidence indicates that by 200 Christianity had a well-established presence in Britain. Although the Roman government was very tolerant of the various religions found in their occupied countries, Christians were sometimes persecuted, especially when they refused to "worship" the emperor.

One of the first Christian martyrs in Britain was Alban, a Roman soldier who was stationed at Verulamium, on the banks of the River Ver north of London. Impressed by his courage and faith, Alban had invited Amphibalus, a Christian, into his home. When soldiers came seeking him, Alban dressed in his guest's cloak, allowing Amphibalus to escape. Taken captive, Alban bravely proclaimed his newly adopted Christian faith, refused to sacrifice to any Roman deity, and was beheaded on June 22 just a few years before Christianity became officially recognized by the Emperor.

Archaeological remains of British Christianity between the years of 300-400 are rare. At Silchester there was a small church on the site of the present parish church. For the rest, the evidence consists mostly of the Chi Rho monogram, XP, the first letters of Christ's name in Greek, which were worked into mosaics or cut into the floors of villas. One example is a simple farm at Lullingstone, which was renovated over several centuries eventually becoming a wealthy villa with two fine mosaics as focal points in the house. Around the year 400 Christians occupied the villa and a room, decorated with Christian symbols and praying figures, was created as a house chapel for the owner's family and close friends. A reconstructed wall painting at the British Museum shows these Christian figures in an attitude of prayer. Chedworth, one of the finest surviving villa sites in Britain, has a dining room that displays the XP or Chi Rho sign.

Constantius Chlorus, Roman commander-in-chief in York in northern Britain, became emperor of the Roman empire in 292. His wife, Helen, had long been a Christian. He was succeeded in 306 by their son, Constantine, who had also served in York. Helen was baptized in 312 and soon afterwards her son granted official status to the Christian faith. It was now possible for Christians to officially organize and build churches in which to worship. Bishops from London, Lincoln, and York were invited in 314 to a council of bishops in Arles, France. The faith had officially arrived in Britain.

The new faith found its followers mostly among the romanized Britons, those who were in contact with the occupiers. The language of the church was overwhelmingly Latin, not Celtic. As a result, only a few pockets of the Christian faith remained when the Roman army withdrew.

The End of Roman Rule in Britain

Faced with the sacking of Rome by Germanic barbarians, Emperor Honorius in 407 called the legionnaires home, thus ending almost 400 years of Roman rule in Britain. Life had been pleasant for the Britons under Roman rule. Now many of their comforts and conveniences, such as well-made roads, hypocausts or central heating generated by hot air passing through flues and channels under the floor, aqueducts for fresh water, and baths such as Aquae Sulis or Bath, would disappear, not to be seen again for hundreds of years. The glory that was Rome in Britain faded into the dark ages.

Although the Roman army officially withdrew, some garrisons whose members now called Britain home remained. During the next two hundred years they were joined by members of the fair-haired Nordic tribes: the Jutes from Sweden, the Saxons from Germany, and the Angles from southern Denmark, who eventually gave their name to a part of Britain, Angle-land (England). The Roman way of life with its law and literacy, its commerce and its cities, disappeared from the British Isles in that overwhelming wave of pagan immigration.

Closing Reflection: Christianity in Britain

Over a period of perhaps a thousand years the migrating Celtic tribes gradually invaded the British Isles bringing the customs, language, arts, and religion that had been developed by them at La Tene, Switzerland. Then in 43 AD the Romans, seeking fame and fortune, landed in Britain. During the occupation, Christianity reached Britain and found followers among the Roman army and those with whom they associated, the romanized Britons. When the army left, small pockets of Christian communities remained behind and survived even as paganism flourished under the invading Nordic tribes. The seeds of faith had been sown. In the next part of this study we will see how those seeds were nurtured and how they grew.

Although Christianity came to the British Isles with the Roman army, it was not to flourish until it was reintroduced through Ireland into Iona, Lindisfarne or Holy Isle, and later through Canterbury. These mission centers were communities in which people were nurtured in the faith and then sent to evangelize the pagan population.

Under Celtic influence, the Christian faith, separated from the continent during the Dark Ages, developed in ways different from the church in Rome. This eventually led to the clash between the two expressions of the faith that left the Celtic model "the way not taken."

Faith Sharing: Paul Writes to Rome

First, I thank my God through Jesus Christ for all of you, because your faith is proclaimed throughout the world. For God, whom I serve with my spirit by announcing the gospel of his Son, is my witness that without ceasing I remember you always in my prayers, asking that by God's will I may somehow at last succeed in coming to you. For I am longing to see you so that I may share with you some spiritual gift to strengthen you—or rather so that we may be mutually encouraged by each other's faith, both yours and mine.

I want you to know, brothers and sisters, that I have often intended to come to you (but thus far have been prevented), in order that I may reap some harvest among you as I have among the rest of the Gentiles. I am a debtor both to Greeks and to barbarians, both to the wise and to the foolish—hence my eagerness to proclaim the gospel to you also who are in Rome. For I am not ashamed of the gospel; it is the power of God for salvation to everyone who has faith, to the Jew first and also to the Greek. For in it the righteousness of God is revealed through faith for faith; as it is written, "The one who is righteous will live by faith." (Romans 1:8–17)

The year is 58 AD and Paul is in Corinth. He has never been to Rome but longs to preach and teach here in the center of the empire, and then perhaps get support for a mission into Spain. He writes that he is excited about the possibility of coming because he has heard of their faith and he wants to be part of their ministry and mission.

Paul begins by complimenting his readers on their faith. He thanks God for them because of their witness, a witness that reaches far and wide, and eventually will extend into Britain. Paul wants to tell the good news to everyone no matter what their education or level of sophistication. With the introduction over, in verses 16–17 Paul states his theme: how can anyone be right with God on the day of judgment? He asserts right standing comes only through faith in Jesus. From that faith springs forgiveness, acceptance, and new life in the Spirit. The rest of his letter explores that theme.

Personal Reflection

1. The Celtic Christians first established small worshiping groups in their homes. Are you involved with a small group ministry? If so, what? If not, why not?

2. How do you stay in touch with friends or family members who live in another city? Letter, phone, e-mail?

Closing Prayer

O God of the morning, Christ of the hills,
O Spirit who all the firmament fills,
O Trinity blest who all goodness wills,
Keep us all our days.[1]

For I perceive the way to life lies here.

Come, pluck up heart, let us neither faint nor fear...

Another profound and ancient truth of pilgrimage is that one's destination is quite likely to not be nearly as important or meaningful as the journey itself.

M. Scott Peck[1]

PART TWO

Relationships: Soul Friends and Thin Places

Christianity came to Britain with the Roman invasion, through its soldiers and those who came with them, their wives, and other civilians such as merchants and educators. The Celts had located in Britain hundreds of years before the Romans came. They created a unique civilization that was to merge with and influence the Roman culture as it developed in Britain.

When the army was recalled to defend Rome, it left behind pockets of Roman-Celtic culture including some Christian congregations. The Celts were driven north into Scotland, west into Wales, south into Cornwall, and to Ireland, Brittany, and the Isle of Man as a result of the Anglo-Saxon invasion. With them went these fledgling churches. Paganism once again reigned in Britain.

But from these scattered pockets of Celtic Christianity arose monasteries, mission centers that were to train missionaries to evangelize their pagan neighbors. Ninian formed a mission center at Whithorn in Scotland to reach the Picts. Pelagius studied theology in Britain and went to Rome for further studies. He is credited with being one of the first Celtic theologians and a reformer much in the tradition of Martin Luther. David established a mission center in Wales. Patrick was called to Ireland to strengthen the struggling Christian witness there. His efforts paved the way for Brigid at Kildare, Ciaran at Clonmacnoise, and Kevin at Glendalough. Columba sailed from Ireland to Scotland where he established a center on Iona from which Aidan was sent to establish a center at Lindisfarne. Aidan commissioned Hilda who eventually established what was to become the largest of the centers in England at Whitby. These were exciting years as the faith continued to spread.

What can we learn from these saints and their sites? Although their unique way of life has disappeared, destroyed by the Vikings and discouraged by the Roman Catholic church, its influence is found in the Reformation and the churches to which it gave birth.

Come now with me on a Celtic Quest along "the way not taken" as we journey with these saints and explore their sites. Learn from them and adapt their ways, for what we are called to do as Christians today and tomorrow is rooted deeply in the Celtic tradition. As we walk with these holy men and women, may they become soul friends or "anamchara" (an-am-cha-ra), mentors guiding us along the way. May the places we visit become "thin places," sites where the wall between earth and heaven is sheer. May you feel some of the peace and joy I felt walking with these soul friends in their thin places. Let's go exploring.

Time Line: Part Two

Dates are often uncertain. c=circa, around that time

360	Martin of Tours (c. 315-397) - mission to Northern France.
397	Ninian (362-432) builds Candida Casa at Whithorn.
400	Pelagius(c. 360-430) arrives in Rome, possibly from Wales.
410	Alaric the Goth sacks Rome; legions withdraw from Britain. Christianity spreads.
432	Patrick (390-461) in Armagh, Ireland.
449	Anglo-Saxons begin invasion of Britain. Brigid (c. 452-524). David (c. 520-589).
544	Clonmacnoise, Ireland. Ciaran (c. 512-545).
563	Columba establishes a monastery on Iona, Scotland. Columba/ Columcille (521-597).
570	Glendalough Monastery, Ireland. Kevin (498-618) becomes abbot.
596	Pope Gregory sends Augustine to Britain.
635	Aidan (d. 651) establishes a monastery on Lindisfarne, Northern Britain.
657	Whitby Monastery, Britain; Hilda (614-680).
664	Council/Synod at Whitby
731	*Ecclesiastical History of the English People* published by the Venerable Bede (673-735).
c. 750	Ardagh chalice.
800	Book of Kells started at Iona, finished at Kells.
1093	Durham Cathedral built between 1093 and 1133.

St. Patrick's
Memorial Church

David's Birth Site

St. Columba's House
in Kells

Iona — High Cross

4
Ninian

When Jesus returned from the Jordan River...
the Spirit led him into the desert.

Luke 4:1

PILGRIM TRAVELS

Friday, July 5
Candida Casa at Whithorn, Scotland

After Iona I drive to Whithorn. My first stop in the morning is Ninian's Cave, located in a ragged cleft in a cliff bordering Physgill Bay outside of Whithorn. Ninian may have used it as a devotional retreat. Crosses are carved on its walls by past pilgrims. Next stop is the Isle of Whithorn to view Ninian's chapel. Built for the pilgrims landing nearby to give thanks for their safe arrival, it may also be where Ninian first landed on his return home.

Whithorn is the cradle of Scottish Christianity, predating Iona by more than 150 years. After a brief chat with the director of the museum and a short introductory film, I visit the museum's fine examples of early Christian standing crosses and headstones. The Latinus stone is the earliest Christian memorial in Scotland. The monk's cells, small wooden structures dating from around 400, are the oldest remains in the monastic settlement that have been unearthed by the dig. A memorial stone was found from that period with the words *Te Domine Laudamus*, "We praise you Lord," confirming that a Christian community existed here. The outline of Ninian's Candida Casa, a mortared stone building with limewashed plaster located on the crown of the hill, has been found among the ruins.

Is it really a pilgrimage if you arrive by plane, train, and car, carrying a Canon camera in an L. L. Bean bag? Contemporary conveniences aside, pilgrimage hasn't changed much since the days of the *Canterbury Tales*. To handle the increased numbers on a spiritual quest today, compromises must be made. Religious sites need to be protected from the thousands of pilgrims who regularly come. Our approach is what really matters. Why are we on this pilgrimage? What will we discover along the way about ourselves?

> My approach to Whithorn is more that of a sightseer than
> a pilgrim. I came to see the site where one of the first, if not
> the first, mission centers was established and to pay homage
> to a man about whom we know very little but enough to know
> that he is the first great saint of the Celtic way. Pictures are
> taken to tell the story some winter night at home. My
> schedule is tight since I need to leave by noon in order to
> cross the causeway to Lindisfarne before the tide covers it.
> When I reach Lindisfarne, I will take time to reflect, to
> contemplate, and to pray.

Ninian (c. 362-432)

In 398, shortly before the Romans withdrew from Britain, Ninian
returned home to the southwest coast of Scotland to establish the first
Christian mission center north of Hadrian's Wall in what was to
become Whithorn. The area had probably been a center of British
trade and power during the Roman occupation, making it a natural
location for the mission.

Born of noble parents, Ninian was educated in Britain and in Rome
where he studied for ten years. After becoming a bishop, he headed
home, possibly stopping along the way at the monastic community
founded by Martin of Tours. Cooperating with the church in his
hometown and its bishop, Ninian created a mission center and school
after Martin's design. The center was reminiscent of a Celtic village
since the monks had their own cells yet participated in communal life.
There he built one of the first stone churches in Scotland, a small
building covered with light-colored plaster, which he called Candida
Casa. *Candida* in Latin means "shining, luminous, glistening white"
and *casa*, "house." The Saxons called it *Hwit herne* or "white house"
which became "Whithorn." The name may have been derived from
the lime with which its walls were painted or perhaps its purpose, to be
a lamp shining the light of faith in a dark world.

Candida Casa drew people from great distances. Kentigern or
Mungo of Glasgow and Finnian of Moville, Ireland, were among the

students who then returned to establish mission centers of their own. These monks traveled throughout Scotland to witness to the Picts, the people who lived there. Celtic cross slabs with the same unique, ringed design have been found both at Whithorn and in parts of northeast Scotland, confirming the extent of Ninian's influence. His monks may have even reached as far as the Shetlands.

Celtic theology is rooted in nature. Ninian's teachings reflect the Celtic theme that God is revealed in the big book (nature) and in the little book (the Bible). His catechism stresses that "the eternal word of God is reflected in every plant and insect, every bird and animal and every man and woman." He held conversations with the Druids, converting many of them to the Christian faith. A strong foundation for the Christian way was laid at Whithorn. Ninian's disciples would build on this in the years that lay ahead.

For more than a thousand years Ninian's tomb was a place of pilgrimage. James IV, who reigned from 1488-1513 and was one of Scotland's best loved monarchs, regularly visited this shrine. In 1581, during the Reformation, the Scottish parliament banned all pilgrimages.

Martin of Tours (c. 315-397)

Martin of Tours was first attracted to the Christian faith at the age of ten but his pagan parents prevented him from being baptized. His father, a Roman soldier, expected him to follow in his footsteps. He served reluctantly in Gaul where he rose to the rank of an officer. When he finally became a Christian, he became a conscientious objector and around 339 left the service.

Martin of Tours radically reshaped the Christian mission by introducing the monastic movement into western Europe. In 360 he formed the first monastery in western Europe in Ligugé. Ten years later, as Bishop of Tours, he established the monastery at Marmoutier, making it his headquarters. He died November 8, 397, close to the time that Ninian was returning home.

Anthony of Egypt (c. 251-356)

Martin had been inspired by the example of the desert Christians who pioneered the monastic movement in Egypt, Palestine, and Syria. One of these was Anthony, the "father of monks," who was born around 251 to Egyptian peasants. As a young adult he heard the words of Jesus: "If you wish to be perfect, go, sell your possessions, and give the money to the poor, and you will have treasure in heaven; then come, follow me" (Matthew 19:21; cf Mark 10:21, Luke 18:22). He took the words personally, worked as a poor laborer near his village for a while, then withdrew into the desert, where he lived alone for twenty years.

After he emerged from that experience, others soon recognized a sense of wholeness or holiness in his life. By 285 a community of disciples had gathered around to learn from him. Toward the end of his life he once again became a hermit in the desert. By the time he died in 356, when he was about 106 years old, the monastic movement had become well-established and widely known. Anthony's experiment with the solitary life, the life of contemplation, attracted western interest through the biography Athanasius wrote about him. Several of the high crosses in Ireland pay homage to Anthony and to Paul of Thebes as pioneers of the monastic movement.

Closing Reflection: Disciplines of the Desert

It is not easy to live the Christian life in a world filled with the temptations of sex, power, and greed. One way of resisting being shaped by them is to withdraw from the world of which they are a part and to create a new world where they are absent. The cry was, "Flee from the world and be saved." Anthony's flight to the desert was his way of creating a better world.

What were some of the disciplines these early Christian communities developed in order to create this new world? Anthony and those who followed him formed small, structured communities in the desert where they learned to live in relationship with each another and with God. Their rule or way of living included long periods of being alone, periods of silence, prayer, and work together for the good of the community.

At the beginning of his ministry, Jesus went into the desert for a long period to be alone with God. During this time he reaffirmed his calling to ministry and mission. We also need periods of being alone with God to reflect on where we have been and where we are going.

Silence was an important discipline in the monastic tradition. Silence forces us to be ourselves, free from distractions. For many, silence is a frightening experience. We avoid it by turning on the TV, flicking on the car radio, or jogging with our Walkman. The early Christians understood that to know God, they must be still. God speaks in the silence, not in the noise that drowns out any contemplative thought. We struggle, as did Anthony, with the sounds that bombard us. Henri Nouwen comments: "In the sayings of the Desert Fathers, we can distinguish three aspects of silence....First, silence makes us pilgrims. Secondly, silence guards the fire within. Thirdly, silence teaches us to speak."[1] Spend some time each day alone in silence. Talk to God and God will talk with you.

The monastic community became a place of conversion as the monks struggled in the desert to live the Christian life. They found strength in community with each other and with God. Our community is the Christian congregation, the place where we learn to live with each other in the family of God. It is there we adopt the spiritual disciplines that transform our lives. Transformed lives flow from a caring ministry.

The core concepts of the monastic tradition include retreating from the world, remaining silent in order to hear what God is calling us to be and do, praying for ourselves and others at all times, working together as a loving community, and sharing the good news.

Anthony's ministry in the desert influenced Martin of Tours, who brought the monastic movement to western Europe. There Ninian discovered it and took it to Scotland. Today we may learn from this movement how to develop the disciplines that will transform our lives and make us more caring disciples of the God we love and serve.

Faith Sharing: Jesus and the Devil

Jesus, full of the Holy Spirit, returned from the Jordan and was led by the Spirit in the wilderness, where for forty days he was tempted by the devil. He ate nothing at all during those days, and when they were over, he was famished. The devil said to him, "If you are the Son of God, command this stone to become a loaf of bread." Jesus answered him, "It is written, 'One does not live by bread alone.'" Then the devil led him up and showed him in an instant all the kingdoms of the world. And the devil said to him, "To you I will give their glory and all this authority; for it has been given over to me, and I give it to anyone I please. If you, then, will worship me, it will all be yours."

Jesus answered him, "It is written, 'Worship the Lord your God, and serve only him.'" Then the devil took him to Jerusalem, and placed him on the pinnacle of the temple, saying to him, "If you are the Son of God, throw yourself down from here, for it is written, 'He will command his angels concerning you, to protect you,' and 'On their hands they will bear you up, so that you will not dash your foot against a stone.'" Jesus answered him, "It is said, 'Do not put the Lord your God to the test.'" When the devil had finished every test, he departed from him until an opportune time. (Luke 4:1–13)

The gospels tell us that at the beginning of his ministry Jesus withdrew into the wilderness for a period of self-reflection just as the desert monks did many years later. Anyone reading the gospels for the first time would want to know if Jesus was God's son, the Messiah or Christ, and how his ministry would prove it. And so the devil says, "If you are God's son…prove it." He suggests three ways that Jesus could prove he was the Messiah. They are to overcome hunger, to strengthen faith, and to create a peaceful world. We are tempted to agree that they seem worthy goals, so why not do them? The devil suggests, "You must be hungry, Jesus. There are many people who experience constant hunger. Feed them and they will follow you. If that doesn't appeal to you, then create a world through force in which people will never be hungry. We can together conquer the kingdoms of the world and bring peace. If you are not willing to do that, then how about helping those who are struggling with their faith? Jump from the temple tower and prove, once and for all, that you are really God's son."

As he began his ministry, Jesus was tempted to place physical before spiritual needs in order to feed the hungry; to bring peace through force rather than love; and to convince those with a shaky faith that he was who he was by performing miraculous acts. Jesus drew on God's word to help his disciples understand why he resisted doing what was expected by the people.

Mature Christians are survivors who know the pitfalls of the journey because they have been down the trail, wrestled with the demons, connected with God, reflected on those experiences, and then shared with others their witness to a loving God. You will find that it is not always easy to be a Christian—but even if it's hard, it's constantly rewarding!

Personal Reflection

1. Consider examples of "the end justifies the means." Are there times when it does? Have you ever justified the way you did something in order to achieve your goal?

Closing Prayer

May the peace of Jesus go with you,
wherever you may be led,
May the Spirit guide you through the wilderness
and help you resist temptation.
May you be renewed for your ministry
by your time in the desert with God.
May you return home rejoicing
at the blessings you have received.

5
Pelagius

We hold that a person is justified by faith.

Romans 3:28

PILGRIM TRAVELS

Thursday, July 11
Portmeirion, Wales

My pilgrimage today is a secular one. The morning begins with a leisurely drive from St. Davids in the southwestern part of Wales along a twisting, winding, coastal road to Portmeirion in northern Wales. After stopping on the way at Aberystwyth for lunch, I arrive at the Old Rectory Inn, a former parsonage. My destination is The Village, the fifty Italianate buildings created by Sir William Ellis located on a secluded wooded peninsula jutting out into Tremadog Bay.

The Prisoner, a television series from the late sixties, was filmed here. Patrick McGoohan played a spy recently resigned from the service who is taken for debriefing to an isolated village where residents are called by numbers not names. The kidnaped former spy resists being debriefed and being identified by his assigned name, Number Six. "I will not be pushed, filed, stamped, indexed, briefed, debriefed or numbered! My life is my own."[1] I still object to being labeled and classified by my social security number rather than my name, and, where I can avoid it, such as on a driver's license, I do so. The "6 in 1" shop where Max carries *Prisoner* memorabilia is my next stop. He wrote a book about the series which he graciously autographs for me. The hotel overlooking the estuary provides a gorgeous view and a five-star dinner.

A place becomes sacred, worthy of respect, when it becomes associated with ideas or persons we respect. *The Prisoner* is meant to provoke, to make people think about the issues of freedom and individuality, something Pelagius also does. The series calls viewers to affirm their individuality and not lose it in the face of a world that seeks to make them conform and to take away their freedom. As pilgrims, we also wrestle with the issues of individuality and conformity. And so we ask, "Can I resist conforming to a culture that rejects the faith I hold?"

It is raining lightly as I hike down the winding path to the hotel. I recall the host of Welsh saints—Pelagius, Illtud, David, and very possibly Patrick—who not only resisted their pagan culture, but sought to share their faith with all of God's children. As I reach the bottom, the sun breaks through over the bay. It is a great day to be alive!

Friday, July 12.
Bangor and St. Deiniol's Library, Wales

The first two weeks of my pilgrimage come to a close with a visit to St. Deiniol's residential library to research the Celtic theologian Pelagius, who may have come from this area.

The skies are clear as I drive through the Snowdonia mountains this morning. Ant-like hikers are climbing all over the hills. In 525 Deiniol built a Celtic monastery in Bangor making it Britain's oldest diocese. Then, after a swift drive along the coast to Hawarden (Har-den), I arrive at St. Deiniol's residential library in time for tea. In the evening, after my first taste of steak and kidney pie, my research on Pelagius in the library begins. There is a stuffy comfortableness about the hallowed halls that reminds me of seminary days. Here is what I discovered.

Pelagius (c. 360-430)

Pelagius, a British monk, is a fourth-century theologian who became a major religious and intellectual force in his time. He was born a Celtic Briton, perhaps in Wales near Chester. His Latin name was Pelagius. The Welsh called him Morgan or Morien. Those who knew him described him as a big man, enthusiastic, strong and stout, well-educated in the Roman/Latin tradition and in the Scriptures.

Pelagius left for Rome around 385 to study law, but God called him to serve as the first major British theologian. He wrote a three-volume book on the Trinity and compiled a collection of Scripture passages relating to Christian practice. Shocked at the low level of morality he found in Rome, he crusaded for higher ethical standards, especially among the clergy.

Pelagius was held in high esteem as a great orator and a competent biblical scholar. His circle of influence grew as people looking for spiritual guidance were attracted to him. Among his dedicated followers was Celestius, a young lawyer, probably also a romanized Celt. Pelagius allowed women into his lectures, ignoring the criticism that they should not be taught to read and interpret the Bible. His call for a higher ethical standard, his cutting-edge theology, and his affirmation of women antagonized some of the clergy of his day.

When Rome fell to Alaric in 410, Pelagius fled to Carthage along with Celestius who remained there with hopes of being ordained by Bishop Aurelius while Pelagius traveled on to meet friends in Jerusalem. When Celestius was denied ordination by an advisory synod in Carthage in 411 over issues of baptism and the nature of infants (original sin), he left for Ephesus where the churches were more supportive and he was ordained there.

Pelagius found a home in Jerusalem where his influence spread through his writings and through personal contact. Opposition to his views grew and a plot to discredit them was hatched in 415. Pelagius was twice acquitted of heresy, first by Bishop John in Jerusalem and later by the Council of Diospolis where his accusers were two discredited bishops, Heros and Lazarus, who had been deposed by the Gallic Church. At that point in time Pelagius was able to produce letters of affection and friendship from Augustine and other church leaders.

Failing to convince other Christian leaders that Pelagius was guilty of heresy, the African bishops convened their own court in Carthage where Pelagius and Celestius were easily tried in absentia and condemned. Appeals to Innocent I, pope from 402-417, to overturn the ruling against Pelagius were rejected. Innocent died soon afterward and was succeeded by Zosimus, a Greek from the Eastern branch of the church. A synod was held in Rome where Celestius argued their defense in person. Impressed by his case and the written Confession of

Faith sent by Pelagius, Zosimus declared the Confession of Faith to be totally orthodox and catholic. He ruled that Pelagius was *absolutae fidei*, unconditionally faithful, excommunicated the accusers, and advised the African bishops, "Love peace, prize love, strive after harmony. For it is written: 'Love thy neighbor as thyself.'" They ignored him.

Having been rejected by the church, the opposing forces turned to the state and the emperor, meeting once again in 418 in a new synod back in Carthage. Their political pressure and exaggerated arguments finally convinced Honorius, the western emperor, to outlaw anyone believing what it was assumed Pelagius believed and to condemn Pelagius as a heretic.

What finally happened to Pelagius? We have no record of him after 420. He may have disappeared into the Egyptian desert where he had friends. Welsh tradition associates Pelagius with the Meirion manuscript and with Wales and Bangor, where he may have returned seeking refuge in a friendly monastery.

The Irish persistently disseminated Pelagian texts, adding their own comments. His call to strive for perfection was highly attractive to the Irish, guiding them in their successful missions in Europe during the Middle Ages. Where Pelagian theology was banned, it is rumored Pelagian texts were copied and sent out under the names of other religious writers such as Jerome and Augustine, a delightful twist of Irish humor, since they had both opposed Pelagius.

Rome as Pelagius Knew It

When Constantine was declared emperor by his soldiers at York in Britain, he returned to Rome with his army. There they fought a series of civil wars, from which he emerged victorious in 324. During his thirteen-year reign Constantine, a fine statesmen of first-class ability, was dedicated to maintaining peace and unity in the empire. When he died in 337, the Empire rapidly disintegrated, and by the end of 406 Gaul had been lost. Legions were recalled to defend Rome, and Britain was abandoned. In 410 Alaric from Gaul sacked Rome.

What happened to the empire? The Roman aristocracy, which had a long and distinguished dedication to public service, was no longer interested in providing leadership. Violence, sex, taverns, and gaming were a way of life. The lower class increasingly depended on welfare and lacked motivation to rise above it. The middle class was increasingly taxed; the upper class obtained favorable assessments and swallowed up the small businesses. (Sound familiar?)

The embracing of Christianity by Constantine and its steady acceptance as the state religion during the fourth century were both its greatest victory and its worst defeat. Constantine extended privileges to the Christian clergy but, rather than reforming the world, they were instead caught up and corrupted by it. The way of the cross, which had led to the rejection of political power, wealth, military command, and loose living, was compromised. Within twenty years, paganism, which in 380 had been virtually intact, was abandoned. Jupiter was out and Jesus was in. The church influenced government decisions. Hard times often breed a sincere and committed faith while prosperity produces lukewarm clergy who put in time. The bishopric of Rome became a prize to be won. A passion for riches attacked the clergy of all ranks, with some living in luxury. The church was now badly divided. It was in this setting that Pelagius practiced his ministry.

Closing Reflection: Theology

Pelagius was a theologian. Theology, the study of God, is something we all do to a greater or lesser degree. Although our pilgrimage may begin in search of a faith, in a quest for something or someone in which to believe, when we connect with God we are on the journey in earnest. Theology seeks to give answers to what God would have us do after conversion. The basic answer is to observe the two Great Commandments and the Great Commission: to love God, ourselves and other people; and to tell the good news. Everything else flows from those teachings.

Contemplation, such as the monks practiced, also helps us know and then do what God would have us do. Try reading aloud a chapter from the Bible; reflecting on what you have read, perhaps writing it down in a journal; then opening your heart and mind to the thoughts God will plant there; and finally considering what you have read, thought, and heard. Contemplation of nature, as well as Scripture, is also a Celtic way of knowing and loving God. Theology tells us that after we say "Yes" to God, we need to move along the path of loving God, loving people, and sharing the faith.

What did Pelagius teach to arouse such a passionate following and such vigorous opposition? By the year 200, traces of Christianity existed in Britain. During the next 200 years, cut off from mainland and eastern Christianity, the church shaped its faith influenced by its Celtic heritage. Raised in this environment, Pelagius became an eloquent defender of an orthodox faith that was rooted in Trinitarian theology. Although a small number of his letters are preserved, none of his major writings has survived. What we know of what he argued is often based on the writings of others. He believed that a gracious God creates us without virtue or vice, that is, a newborn baby starts with a clean slate. God creates us in his image as persons with individual souls, free wills, and the conscience to monitor our choices. Pelagius never taught the doctrine of original sin and denied sin was inherited from Adam. He wrote, "Everything good and everything evil…is done by us, not born with us."

Pelagius affirmed that it is our nature to turn to God and we are able to do so. He did not believe in double predestination, teaching that a fair and just God would not make two groups, one saved and one damned. We all have a choice and grace means we all have a chance. We are judged good or evil by our own success or failure in following God's law in conscience. "The person who is prepared to toil and strive to avoid sin and to walk in the commandments of God on behalf of his own salvation, is granted by God the possibility of so doing."

Pelagius was the first major British commentator on biblical texts. Commenting on love, he wrote: "Charity is manifest in four ways: love of God, love of ourselves, love of neighbors, and love of enemies. We are called to love God more than we love ourselves, to love our neighbor as ourselves, and our enemy as our neighbor."

Pelagius stressed public morality and social justice. His condemnation of the rich and those who were evil contributed greatly to the opposition he unjustly received. Like Paul before him and Luther after him, Pelagius recognized that sin is pervasive and needs to be challenged. He believed we are saved by "justification by faith," a banner taken up by Luther a thousand years later, through baptism, by reason of the ministry of Jesus. He created a theology that affirmed that after baptism, we are given the duty to keep the divine law of a loving God.

Pelagius stressed human freedom, teaching that while emotions are neither good nor bad, we are responsible for our actions resulting from them. He believed we are to seek guidance for the Christian life from the teachings of Jesus, from our conscience, and from prayer.

In 597 Gregory sent a mission to root out Pelagian theology in Britain but his ideas remained popular. The core of Pelagian thought lived on in Celtic Britain and Ireland. Twentieth-century theologian Karl Barth characterized the people of Britain as "incurably Pelagian." The debate continues today within the church over many of the same issues he challenged: authority and freedom, and the role of women in the church.

Faith Sharing:
God's Way of Accepting People

But now, apart from law, the righteousness of God has been disclosed, and is attested by the law and the prophets, the righteousness of God through faith in Jesus Christ for all who believe. For there is no distinction, since all have sinned and fall short of the glory of God; they are now justified by his grace as a gift, through the redemption that is in Christ Jesus, whom God put forward as a sacrifice of atonement by his blood, effective through faith. He did this to show his righteousness, because in his divine forbearance he had passed over the sins previously committed; it was to prove at the present time that he himself is righteous and that he justifies the one who has faith in Jesus. Then what becomes of boasting? It is excluded. By what law? By that of works? No, but by the law of faith. For we hold that a person is justified by faith apart from works prescribed by the law. (Romans 3:21–28)

Paul tells us the good news that God has dealt with our sin via the death and resurrection of Jesus. "Justification by faith" is a metaphor used only by Paul who borrowed it from the court system of his day to describe to his readers what it means to be saved. If during a trial, the accused is found "innocent" or "not guilty" by the judge, then that person is declared "justified" or legally in the right. Justification by faith means we are in a right relationship with God through faith in Jesus. It is a doctrine that declares what it means to be a Christian.

Personal Reflection

1. What are some of the major controversies that seem to divide Christians today? Which one affects you personally? Are any of these controversies a barrier to community in your family or parish? If so, how can this be resolved?

Closing Prayer

God be in my head, and in my understanding;
God be in mine eyes, and in my looking;
God be in my mouth, and in my speaking;
God be in my heart, and in my thinking;
God be at mine end, and at my departing.

Sarum Primer, 1558

6
Patrick

Go to the people of all nations and make them my disciples.
Baptize them in the name of the Father,
the Son, and the Holy Spirit,
and teach them to do everything I have told you.

Matthew 28:19–20

PILGRIM TRAVELS

In Ireland

After visiting sites in Scotland, northern England, and Wales, I fly to Ireland where I will stay at Trinity College in Dublin while visiting sites related to Patrick, Brigid, Ciaran, and Kevin.

Saturday, July 20
Armagh or Ard Macha or Macha's Hill

Armagh is named after the legendary Queen Macha who built Fort Navan nearby. Patrick made Armagh the center of his mission and it remains the spiritual capital of Ireland today. The elegant Armagh tourist center tells the tale of Patrick through the latest audiovisual forms. St. Patrick's Cathedral is located on the site of Patrick's original church. The High King of Ireland, Brian Boru, is said to be buried near the church.

Armagh lies in Ulster in Northern Ireland, a troubled place. Conflicts over parade routes a few weeks before have heightened the tension. Economical and political pressures may pave the way for a peaceful solution. Somehow the legacy of the past, the old prejudices and attitudes, must be overcome. The church has a role to play in moving the people of Ireland toward reconciliation rather than revenge. Christians affirm a basic core of beliefs which include forgiveness and striving for peace. Patrick would be pleased if his adopted people could reconcile their differences.

Sunday, July 21
Downpatrick and Saul

Farmland surrounds me as I go down a country road to Saul where Patrick began his ministry in 432. His first church there was a barn which in Irish is called "Sabhall." Fifteen hundred years later, in 1932, St. Patrick's Memorial Church, a lovely little chapel with a standing tower, was erected on the crown of the hilltop where Patrick is said to have made his first converts. It is a peaceful setting with a magnificent view of the valley. It is pleasant to consider that Patrick might be buried here.

In the evening people are streaming into a church across the street from the Kilmorey Arms Hotel in Kilkeel where I am staying. Joining the crowd for the evening service, I am caught up in a joyful celebration of heartwarming prayers and inspiring hymns led by a choir of more than fifty. Thank you, Lord. I end the day truly blessed!

Tuesday, July 23
Cashel

High on a hill lies the fortress of Cashel. The kings of Munster reigned here from 370 to 1101. Patrick is said to have visited the site in 450 to baptize King Aengus. The tale is told that during the ceremony he accidentally stuck his sharply pointed pastoral staff in the king's foot. The king, believing this to be part of the ritual, stoically bore it. Patrick apologized profusely afterwards. The fortress was donated to the church in 1101 and became a cathedral. The magnificent ruins on the Rock of Cashel are an impressive reminder of earlier days and are well worth a visit.

Patrick (c. 390-461)

When the Roman army left, Britain was exposed to the attacks of the Angles and Saxons on the east and the Irish Celts on the west. Slavery was a thriving institution. Small Irish parties would sail in at night, locate an isolated house, kidnap some sleeping children, and quickly retreat. Patrick or Magonus Sucatus Patricius was sixteen when he was captured in one of these raids and sold to a local king who put him to work as a shepherd in the Antrim hills. Alone with the sheep, or possibly cattle, often cold and hungry, he survived for six years in his personal wilderness. Patrick had been part of the romanized Briton middle class living on his father's estate at Bannaven Taburniae, a village most likely set on the banks of the Severn. His father, Calpurnius, was a deacon and his grandfather, Potitus, a Christian priest. Patrick had a good classical education which included a knowledge of the Christian religion. Although he had little faith, if any, in God, found priests foolish, and did not follow the faith of his grandfather, he often turned to God in prayer now that he was alone in the wilderness. During his years there he moved from being a young agnostic to a holy man ready to do God's work.

Called in a dream to return home, he became a fugitive on the run, traveling more than 200 miles to the coast to find a ship to take him to Britain. A cargo ship refused him passage, but when they were ready to sail, allowed him to come aboard. Patrick witnessed to the crew, more than once rescuing his companions from starvation by promising God would provide if they only believed. He eventually made it home to loving parents who encouraged him to settle down and stay. But Patrick saw a vision and heard a call from Ireland, "We beg you to come and walk once more among us."

Patrick probably spoke Welsh, basic Latin, and Irish (which he had learned as a slave), so he had the language skills for the mission. He sharpened his theological knowledge at a monastery. Several claim him. It may have been Ninian's Candida Casa or the island monastery of Lerins. He was ordained in 430, became a bishop, and was sent by the British church as a missionary to the Christians in Ireland in 432, where he eventually took up residence in Armagh as bishop in 433.

We know very little of his actual movements in Ireland and not much of what he did there. Among his first converts was said to be a local chieftain, Dichu, who gave Patrick a barn for holding services. At the close of his mission to Ireland, Patrick could look back with satisfaction on what he had accomplished. His opposition caused the Irish slave trade to disappear during his lifetime. From his center in Armagh, he evangelized northern Ireland, extending his mission by ordaining clergy throughout northern, eastern, and central Ireland. He converted and baptized a vast number of people, encouraging many to become monks and nuns.

Patrick was an evangelist who shared his faith with the pagans around him. Tradition sets the date of his death as March 17, 461, although that is not certain. He is probably buried at Saul or perhaps Downpatrick.

His Writings

Near the end of his life Patrick wrote *A Letter to Coroticus* and his *Confessions*, the two authentic documents of his which are still in existence. Both documents affirm God's presence and providence in Patrick's life. (The "Breastplate," a prayer sometimes attributed to Patrick, is written in his style although he did not write it.)

Letter to Coroticus

Although slavery may have disappeared where Patrick had some influence, it remained strong in northern Britain where Coroticus, a Christian warlord, was leading raiding parties into Ireland. He carted off some of Patrick's converts, and was "distributing baptized girls for a price" into slavery. Patrick angrily wrote to him condemning the raids. He wanted him to know that he had established the Christian faith in Ireland and that they were attacking their brothers and sisters in Christ. Frequently quoting from the Bible to support his decision, Patrick, as bishop, directly and explicitly excommunicated Coroticus and his supporters. The impact of the letter was such that copies have survived.

The Confessio or Confession

Toward the end of his mission rumors were circulated to destroy Patrick, accusing him of misusing mission funds that had been entrusted to him. Perhaps it was the letter to Coroticus that stirred the British attacks. In response, he wrote his famous autobiographical *Confession*, defending his mission and revealing a very spiritual and humble person. Like Paul, he told of traveling extensively and ordaining clergy to serve the faith communities he started. These mission centers in Ireland and Great Britain, isolated from the continent during the Dark Ages, eventually evolved into a unique form of Celtic-influenced Christianity.

> I am Patrick, a sinner, most unlearned, the least of all the faithful, and utterly despised by many. My father was Calpornius, a deacon, son of Potitus, a priest, of the village of Bannaven Taburniae; he had a county seat (estate) nearby, and there I was taken captive. I was then about sixteen years of age. I did not know the true God. I was taken into captivity to Ireland with many thousands of people—and deservedly so, because we turned away from God, and we did not keep his commandments, and did not obey our priests, who used to remind us of our salvation. And the Lord brought over us the wrath of his anger and scattered us among many nations, even unto the utmost part of the earth, where now my littleness is placed among strangers.[1]

He wrote in his defense, "I have baptized many thousands of people, but never asked as much as a halfpenny in return." Patrick included a doctrinal statement in his confession, which he later called a *mensura fidei trinitatis* or "rule of faith of the trinity."

He spent the last thirty years of his life in a mission to the people of Ireland, baptizing and teaching, fulfilling the commission the risen Jesus gave his disciples.

Myths and Legends

In the years following his death, many myths and legends about Patrick developed in order to counteract the ancient myths and legends of pagan Celtic superheroes. Patrick's biography, written some four hundred years after his death, did little to belie these stories, encouraging the image of Patrick as a superhero. Some of the myths which have persisted to this day include:

1. There are no snakes in Ireland because Patrick drove them out.
2. Patrick used the shamrock to explain the Trinity: Father, Son, and Holy Spirit. (He may have; we really don't know.)
3. On the hill of Slane in County Meath he lit a fire to challenge the power of the Druids on the nearby Hill of Tara.

Closing Reflection: Mission Centers

The Irish tended to form small, independent villages rather than larger organized communities such as cities or towns. The Roman diocesan system of appointing a bishop to organize parishes struggled in the Irish setting, while the monastic system thrived, eventually dotting the countryside with more than 800 mission centers. These monasteries were small villages where men and women worked, trained, and prayed together. Peter Harbison questions whether Patrick ever tried to set up a diocesan system in Ireland as some have suggested, since he "may have had to put more energy into conversion than organization."[2] Finnian of Clonard in County Meath was trained by Ninian at Candida Casa. His disciples include Columba from Iona, Ciaran from Clonmacnoise, and Brendan the Navigator from Clonfert. And so the faith spread.

A mission center usually was organized around a charismatic figure who lived the faith. Someone would hear the call of God to go out into his or her own personal "desert" and become a hermit for a period of time. An example of this would be Kevin at Glendalough. These hermits attracted others who would come to learn from them. Their disciples would build simple huts in the forest and eventually a chapel and thus a mission center was formed. These holy men and women would support each other in community, learn the faith and practice it, and then evangelize the area around them. It was a simple life. They provided a ministry of hospitality, a place for weary travelers and the sick.

Each community drew up their rules for living together. The abbots were primarily pastors or spiritual advisors, although they also often functioned as administrators. Individual monks and nuns would occasionally break off from the community and establish new mission centers, gathering disciples around them. At Iona, Columba limited the number at the mission center to 150. When that was reached, a leader and twelve other monks would leave to form another center somewhere else. Although many of these mission centers were small, twelve or more disciples in all, some grew to include thousands of men and women becoming the largest settlements in Ireland. Thus, Christianity expanded throughout Ireland.

Parish consultant Lyle Schaller writes that the more effective churches in the next century will be "organized around three central foci—(a) worship, (b) teaching, and (c) missions."[3] Does that sound familiar? Of course it does! The Celts were doing it 1500 years ago. Churches need to become mission centers in which we worship, teach disciples, and witness in our communities.

Faith Sharing:
The Great Commission

Now the eleven disciples went to Galilee, to the mountain to which Jesus had directed them. When they saw him, they worshiped him; but some doubted. And Jesus came and said to them, "All authority in heaven and on earth has been given to me. Go therefore and make disciples of all nations, baptizing them in the name of the Father and of the Son and of the Holy Spirit, and teaching them to obey everything that I have commanded you. And remember, I am with you always, to the end of the age." (Matthew 28:16–20)

Celtic theology emphasizes the Trinity, the Christian doctrine that affirms our understanding of God. It affirms God as "Father, Son, and Holy Spirit." It may seem a simple doctrine but it is the product of a long and serious debate within the life of the church. Although the word Trinity does not appear in the Scriptures, the idea was already forming in the early church and was expressed here in Matthew and in Paul's letters.

What the doctrine of the Trinity proclaims for all to hear is that God is one although we may experience God in different ways. We may perceive God primarily as Creator, architect of all around us; or as Jesus, loving and saving us; or as Spirit, sustaining and strengthening us. In each experience it is the same God—not three, but one—one divine presence. The bottom line is not belief in the Trinity or any other theological doctrine, but simply that God loves us and we experience that love in different ways. We attempt to describe these ways in order to communicate to others what we are experiencing.

We may not understand the Trinity, but if we wait to understand every experience in life before we enjoy or are blessed by its benefits, then we may never fly in an airplane, use electricity, take an aspirin, enjoy a sunset, or experience the love of a friend. All these and much more in life we do not completely understand; we simply believe, accept, and are blessed by them.

Personal Reflection

1. Patrick was an evangelist committed to sharing his faith with others. Who are some of your friends and acquaintances who don't feel the love of God in their lives? How can you share the good news of God's love with them?

Closing Prayer

This ancient hymn—known variously as the *Lorica Sancti Patritii*, "The Deer's Cry" or *Faeth Fiada*, or St. Patrick's Breastplate—was written in Old Irish in the eighth century, too late for it to be actually written by Patrick. Here is a portion of this prayer:

> *For my shield this day I call:*
> *A mighty power: the Holy Trinity!*
> *Affirming threeness, Confessing oneness*
> *In the making of all Through love....*[4]

7

Brigid
of Kildare

Faith in Christ Jesus is what makes each of you equal with each other, whether you are a Jew or a Greek, a slave or a free person, a man or a woman.

Galatians 3:28

PILGRIM TRAVELS

Saturday, July 20

Stopping at a small parklike area dedicated to Brigid provides me with one of the more moving experiences of my pilgrimage. A stream of clear, fresh water flows through the grounds. Water is believed to have healing powers when associated with someone such as Brigid so the ill come here to be healed by a combination of water and prayer. As I stand quietly in the park, an older couple comes to participate in the ritual of healing. He sits on a bench while she scoops water from the stream and places it in a small hollow of a large stone nearby. He is recovering from recent eye surgery. They have come to Brigid's holy well for several weeks now, placing water in the rock, then wetting a handkerchief and placing it on his eyes, and praying. His sight is better he believes. Their faith in the potential for healing and their love of each other is a heartwarming experience. They continue to affirm the love of God in their lives.

Even though there are times when the streams of life do not flow our way, we are blessed. During my pilgrimage my flight was canceled and luggage misrouted, Ireland had border tensions, my visit to Monasterboice's high crosses was canceled and had to be rescheduled, and since I was last there, Durham Cathedral has prohibited cameras. Despite that, almost everything I hoped to do, I have done. The people along the way have shown me God's love. I have made new friends and my health has held despite turning sixty and fearing postpolio syndrome. God has been good!

Brigid or Brigit of Kildare (c. 452-524)

Because women were accepted and honored in the Celtic culture, remarkable women such as Brigid rose to positions of leadership within the Christian community. In her, the Celtic and Christian cultures intertwined for she was born, in the middle of the fifth century, to a Christian slave woman and a Druid master.

Brigid, one of Patrick's converts, founded a famous double monastery at Kildare or Cill Dara, which means "church of the oak wood." When the Celts became Christians, they often incorporated many elements of their religion into their new-found faith. The Kildare monastery is located in an oak grove, where the Druids would have located a worship site. Until the dissolution of the monastery, an eternal flame was kept burning.

Kildare was led jointly by an abbot and an abbess. Men and women, although living separately, sometimes shared the same eating place. Kildare, known for its hospitality to the poor and sick, eventually became the largest monastic settlement in Ireland. Brigid served as abbess of the community until her death. As high abbess her activities ranged from healing services to hearing confessions, ordaining clergy to celebrating Mass. What pleased God the most, said Brigid, was "true faith in the Lord with a pure heart, a simple life with piety, and generosity with charity."

In pre-Christian times Bridget or Bride (pronounced Breed), had been a very important Celtic divinity, the earth goddess of fertility and healing. Rivers and springs were named for her. Worship of the goddess Bridget was eventually transferred to Brigid and legends developed around her. During the Middle Ages she became the patron saint of travelers and pilgrims. St. Brigid's Cross, often made of straw, is traditionally believed to ward off evil and to keep the homestead safe.

Along with Patrick and Columba, Brigid is honored as a leader in the early church in Ireland. Today she is a model for women in the church everywhere.

The Brigid Legends

As with all the Celtic saints, fact and fiction are intertwined. Here are some of the legends within which some fact may be found.

Giving All to the Poor

Following her conversion, Brigid angered her father by continually giving away his wealth and property to the poor and needy. In desperation he decided to sell her to Dunlaing, the king of Leinster, to work in his fields. When he arrived at the castle, he left his sword with Brigid in the chariot so that he might approach the king unarmed. When a leper came by asking for alms, she gave him the sword.

Inside the castle, the king spoke to Brigid's father. "Why do you want to sell your daughter?" the king asked. "She is selling all I have and giving it to the poor," he replied.

When the king had finished speaking with the father, he called in Brigid to talk with her. In doing so, he discovered she had given away her father's sword. When asked why, she replied, "The Virgin's Son knows if I had your power, with all your wealth, and with all your land, I would give them all to the Lord."

The king then rejected the father's offer of service noting Brigid was too good to be a servant.

Call to Ministry

Brigid and several other young women were called to become nuns. During the ceremony she was the last to appear before Bishop Mel who mistakenly read the form of ordaining a bishop over her. He commented afterward, "No powers have I in this matter. What is done is done. God gave this honor to her beyond that of every woman." Thus, Irish tradition pictures her as the first woman priest having been ordained by a bishop.

Kildare

Brigid, along with the other nuns then founded a monastery. Ailill, son of Dunlaing, donated the wood and workers to build the great house at Kildare. Kings needed monastic support in those days as much as monasteries needed royal patronage.

Wise Sayings

When her driver, attempting a shortcut, overturned their cart, Brigid rose from the wreck, dusted herself off, and remarked "Shortcuts make broken bones."

Anamchara or soul friend

A soul friend or *anamchara* is someone with whom you can share your life and seek advice. The Druids pioneered the way of the soul friend. Ian Bradley comments in his excellent book, *The Celtic Way*: "Modern experts in the field of spiritual counseling and clinical psychology are coming to see the advantages of this Celtic model of pastoral care which faced up to the need we all have for regularly unburdening our souls...."[1]

Brigid was a counselor to the men and women of the area who were called to ministry and mission. Once, when eating in the dining hall, she inquired,

"Well, young cleric, do you have a soul friend?"

"I have," he replied.

"Let us sing his requiem," advised Brigit, "for he is dead. I saw, when you had eaten half your food, that it went directly to your body, because you were without a head. I believe your soul friend has died, because anyone without a soul friend is like a body without a head."

Celtic Rune of Hospitality

Brigid and the mission center at Kildare were known, as many of the centers were, for their hospitality.

I saw a stranger yestereen, I put food in the eating place,
drink in the drinking place, music in the listening place.
And in the sacred name of the Triune
he blessed myself and my house, my cattle and my dear ones.
And the lark said in her song: often, often, often,
goes the Christ in the stranger's guise.[2]

Closing Reflection: Women in the Church

The role of women in the church has never been free from controversy. Even today, most church bodies are discussing how best to utilize women in their mission and ministry. It has been and continues to be a sensitive area.

The New Testament tells us that ministry in the early church was effective because the Holy Spirit gave gifts to all of God's people. Any person could exercise ministry who was called and gifted by God and affirmed by the congregation. Some were set apart in leadership positions and some were assigned specific tasks to accomplish, but all had some form of ministry to perform.

The modern debates over women in the ministry often refuse to consider the examples found in the New Testament. Jesus included women within his circle of disciples, teaching them to share in his ministry. Women were the first to see Jesus at his resurrection and to tell others about it. Women were part of the first church in Jerusalem. They were part of the group who waited in Jerusalem for the coming of the Spirit. Women helped Paul start churches and keep them growing. The foundation for women in ministry is laid by Paul in his letter to the Galatian/Celtic churches. "Faith in Christ Jesus is what makes each of you equal with each other, whether you are a Jew or a Greek, a slave or a free person, a man or a woman" (Galatians 3:28).

These three traditional pairings reflect the three basic hostile social areas during Paul's day. Although God created differences between male and female, sexual differentiation should not determine how one participates in the church. Paul mentions nine women by name who were coworkers with him in the gospel ministry.

The full evidence of Scripture calls us to rethink some prejudicial, patriarchal traditions and to reaffirm with clarity and conviction the biblical basis for the full participation of women in the ministries of the church. The ministry of the church belongs to the whole people of God. The number of women in seminaries has increased dramatically and many in various traditions are taking degrees that prepare them for an ordained ministry.

We nurture our daughters in the faith. When they respond by committing their lives to following Jesus wherever he may lead them, we should be supportive of their call. Women represent an increasingly large proportion of the trained and competent leadership available to the church. They have a new image of themselves and they will insist that their leadership be recognized. Let us be supportive of their call by God to ministry.

Faith Sharing: God's Family

For in Christ Jesus you are all children of God through faith. As many of you as were baptized into Christ have clothed yourselves with Christ. There is no longer Jew or Greek, there is no longer slave or free, there is no longer male and female; for all of you are one in Christ Jesus. And if you belong to Christ, then you are Abraham's offspring, heirs according to the promise.

My point is this: heirs, as long as they are minors, are no better than slaves, though they are the owners of all the property; but they remain under guardians and trustees until the date set by the father. So with us; while we were minors, we were enslaved to the elemental spirits of the world. But when the fullness of time had come, God sent his Son, born of a woman, born under the law, in order to redeem those who were under the law, so that we might receive adoption as children. And because you are children, God has sent the Spirit of his Son into our hearts, crying, "Abba! Father!" So you are no longer a slave but a child, and if a child then also an heir, through God. (Galatians 3:26—4:7)

The Jews and Greeks of the first century were poles apart. Jewish contempt for the non-Jew was intense. In their opinion, Gentiles or non-Jews had been created by God as fuel for the fires of hell. For that barrier to fall was simply incredible. Although some sixty million slaves virtually ran the Roman Empire, they were generally regarded as mere things, without rights, subject to any whim of their masters. This was another barrier broken down by Jesus.

A woman had few if any rights in either first-century Judaism or in the Greek-Roman culture. She belonged to her father or to her husband and he could treat her as he chose, including divorcing her with ease. This barrier Jesus also removes so that in the same way a non-Jew or a slave could exercise leadership in the church, so too could women.

In morning prayer a Jewish man thanked God that he had not been made a Gentile, a slave, or a woman. He was thanking God that as a man he was not disqualified as they were from certain religious privileges. Paul reverses this prayer. The traditional distinctions are finished. In Jesus all are equal, all are one. This was a radical principle in Jesus' time as it is in ours; a dream of what will be. There are still those who are fuel for the fires of hell who keep the dream from coming true.

Personal Reflection

1. Do women have leadership positions in your church? Are any closed to them? Would you be supportive if your church called a woman as its pastor or as a priest?
2. How have you dealt with inclusive language issues? How has your church? Do you use inclusive language and images of God in your own prayer? Why or why not?

Closing Prayer

Here is a table grace associated with Brigid:

God bless the poor,
God bless the sick,
And bless our human race.
God bless our food,
God bless our drink,
All homes, O God, embrace.[3]

8
David

When you accepted the message, you followed our example and the example of the Lord.

1 Thessalonians 1:6

PILGRIM TRAVELS

Tuesday, July 9
St. Davids

A stop in Wales on the way to St. Davids is Llantwit Major or Llanilltud Fawr, meaning the "great church of Illtud," where Illtud founded his mission center. God has been worshiped here for more than 1,500 years making it one of Christianity's oldest sites in Great Britain and one of Britain's oldest centers of learning.

My destination for the day is St. Davids or Tyddewi, the House of David. It is a village of 1,500 people with one town square and a few side roads, but if you have a cathedral you must be a city—thus it is Britain's smallest city. Nona Rees, sub-librarian at the cathedral, is my charming guest this evening for dinner as we discuss tomorrow's schedule.

Wednesday, July 10

In the morning we drive out to St. Non's Bay and the traditional site of David's birth. A small spring or holy well, which is said to have emerged when he was born, still flows freely here. With Nona's help, we struggle down into the field where an abandoned thirteenth-century chapel lies in ruins. There is a simple cross-inscribed stone in the southeast corner, which dates from the seventh century. The standing stones around the edge indicate the field may have been an early center for religious observances.

Next we visit the ruins of a sixteenth-century chapel overlooking Ramsey Sound that may have been built on the site of a Celtic oratory. Justinian, a friend of David, was a hermit born in Brittany. Legend records that Justinian was murdered on Ramsey Island, walked across the Sound with his head in his arms, and laid himself to rest on the spot marked by this chapel.

The lower slopes of Carn Llidi near Whitesands Bay where David first established a monastery, Ty Gwyn, have a lovely view. The bluestones of Stonehenge came from the nearby Preseli Hills and there are hundreds of Celtic sites in the area. Wildflowers and sea birds abound making this a great vacation spot for anyone interested in birds.

The magnificent cathedral was built on what was believed to be the site of the original monastery by the Norman bishop Bernard. Pilgrims flocked here during the Middle Ages; two pilgrimages here equaled one to Rome. They continue to come. Nona has recently written a booklet on the cathedral's misericords. After lunch I wander around the grounds taking pictures of the cathedral both inside and out. It has some very striking modern stained glass. Near the cathedral are the ruins of the Bishop's Palace built between 1328-1347.

With two days here, the pace, brisk since leaving Iona, is more relaxed. David was a highly disciplined individual committed to a simple life-style. We would all probably live longer and enjoy life more if we could form a simple basic rule for our lives that combined good food, continued learning, and a right relationship with God.

David or Dewi (c. 520-589)

David (Dewi in Welsh) became a Celtic monk, abbot, bishop, and the patron saint of Wales. His mother, Non, the daughter of a local chieftain, was raped by Sant, the son of another nobleman. She was probably a baptized Christian. Tradition indicates she fled to Brittany, died there, and is buried in Dirinon.

After his education by Paulinus, David left the area for ministry possibly in Ireland, but probably in the eastern area of England. Eventually returning home, he founded a monastery at Glyn Rhosyn, "valley of the little marsh," an ideal location on the intersection of the north-south and east-west major sea routes. Such mission centers were usually surrounded by a wall within which were several huts, an oratory for preaching and worship, and a high cross. Life in a monastic community was often simple and hard. David's rule prohibited alcoholic beverages and stressed a basic diet of water, bread, and vegetables, especially wild leeks. His advice was, "Brothers and sisters, be cheerful and keep your faith and belief, and do the little things that you have heard and seen through me."

David was attractive, about six feet tall, and very strong. He spoke Latin and early forms of Welsh and Irish. As a scholar, he attracted students from as far away as Ireland, Cornwall, and Brittany. The traditional day of his death is March 1, 589, which is now the National Day of Wales. March 2 honors his mother, Non. David was buried near the beautiful twelfth-century Norman cathedral that bears his name. It is a grand monument to David's ministry.

Illtud

Before David there was Illtud who founded a church, monastery, and university circa 500 in the quiet little Welsh valley near the sea where Llantwit Major is located today. He came from Brittany to southern Wales where legend suggests he may have formerly been a knight in King Arthur's army. While serving the king of Glamorgan, he was converted by Cadoc, a Christian hermit, became a disciple of Germanus of Auzerre at the monastery founded by Cassian near Marseilles, and was eventually ordained (c. 445). His mission center attracted scholars where an education equipped them and a calling challenged them. Many returned home as monks and missionaries spreading the Christian faith in their countries. Alumni include Gildas, who compiled the first Welsh history, and Samson, who eventually became the abbot of the monastery.

The practice of unceasing praise, or *laus perennis*, was taken literally. The community was divided into twenty-four groups, each responsible for an hour of prayer daily. Although nothing remains of the original buildings, the memory of Illtud's mission center lives on in the church there.

The Misericords of St. Davids

Medieval cathedrals were built to provide space for worship by the

crowds of people who would attend on holy days. Most of the daily
worship by the cathedral community, however, took place in the choir
area which was almost like a separate room. Originally participants
stood during the services. Although the aged and infirm priests at first
used crutches, eventually hinged seats were built in the stalls. These
misericords, "mercy" seats, have a small ledge on the top of them so
that when the seat is up, one is supported while standing.

Although the woodcarvers skillfully praised God through their art
in the rest of the cathedral, they were allowed to carve a variety of
designs out of public view under these seats. The misericords are a
treasure trove of serious and satirical woodcarvings that are a delight
to view. St. Davids cathedral has an interesting variety of them. Nona
Rees dates the misericords of St. Davids to around 1470. My favorite
was the "Owl in the Ivy" about which she writes, "This delightful owl,
perched in luxuriant ivy, is probably a barn owl. It has a smooth, round
head and was known as a 'chouette' in medieval France. It was a
popular bird and, because people believed that its eyes had a luminous
force that could dissolve shadows, this owl became linked to Jesus."[1]

Closing Reflection:
A Rule for Living the Christian Way

The word disciple means to follow the discipline of a master or teacher.
Jesus had disciples who followed him and disciplined their lives in the
light of his teachings. In the Celtic tradition each monastic community
under the leadership of its spiritual director, the abbot, developed its
own "rule" or "way of living" in order to discipline its life together.

You may have felt the call to follow Jesus as a disciple. Afterward
you may have wondered, what do I do now? How do I discipline my
life? Here are seven disciplines for Christian living that are part of the
Christian tradition.

1. *Worship.* The disciple worships regularly with other Christians not
only to praise God but also to witness to others that worship is an
important part of the Christian life.

2. *Community.* The disciple meets regularly with other disciples in
small groups, growing in mutual care for other members of the family
of God.

3. *Devotion.* The disciple reads the Bible and prays regularly.

4. *Ministry.* The disciple discovers his or her unique calling to a ministry. As Christians, we are all called to some form of a ministry; the list is endless. Disciples care, performing acts of service in God's name.

5. *Giving.* The disciple cheerfully contributes to the support of the church's mission by sharing a definite portion of time, talent, and income.

6. *Witness.* The disciple, without apologies, shares with family, friends, and neighbors what it personally means to follow Jesus.

7. *Study.* The disciple reads materials, books or magazines, that will deepen faith.

Faith Sharing:
The Faith of the Thessalonians

Paul, Silvanus, and Timothy, To the church of the Thessalonians in God the Father and the Lord Jesus Christ: Grace to you and peace. We always give thanks to God for all of you and mention you in our prayers, constantly remembering before our God and Father your work of faith and labor of love and steadfastness of hope in our Lord Jesus Christ.

For we know, brothers and sisters beloved by God, that he has chosen you, because our message of the gospel came to you not in word only, but also in power and in the Holy Spirit and with full conviction; just as you know what kind of persons we proved to be among you for your sake. And you became imitators of us and of the Lord, for in spite of persecution you received the word with joy inspired by the Holy Spirit, so that you became an example to all the believers in Macedonia and in Achaia.

For the word of the Lord has sounded forth from you not only in Macedonia and Achaia, but in every place your faith in God has become known, so that we have no need to speak about it. For the people of those regions report about us what kind of welcome we had among you, and how you turned to God from idols, to serve a living and true God, and to wait for his Son from heaven, whom he raised from the dead—Jesus, who rescues us from the wrath that is coming.
(1 Thessalonians 1:1–10)

This letter, written to real people in a real place, was sent by Paul from Corinth in the year 51 to a gathering of Christians in the urban city of Thessalonica. What Paul said is still fresh and challenging today because the issues are similar. Because this letter is generally regarded as one of the earliest in the New Testament, it provides an early account of life in the church.

Grace and peace used together will become Paul's hallmark. Shalom/peace (Hebrew) and chara/grace (Greek) were both common greetings. Paul combines them as he greets his mixed audience. "Grace to you and peace!"

The rest of the chapter tells of how these converts came to trust in the good news. When we realize God loves us, we respond to that love. When we accept the gospel, we become disciples following the example of Paul and of Jesus. We show in our life-style that we love God thus becoming examples for others. People may not know Jesus, but if they see him in our lives they will want to know him.

Personal Reflection

1. Those who are on a pilgrimage, searching for a way of life that will bring them closer to God, often practice the seven disciplines listed above. Are any of these disciplines part of your spiritual life? Which one do you need to concentrate on? How will you do that?

Closing Prayer

May God the Father bless you,
May God the Son heal you,
May God the Holy Spirit enlighten you.
May God protect you from harm and
grant you salvation.
May he shine on your heart and
lead you to eternal life.
And the blessing of God almighty,
Father, Son and Holy Spirit,
come upon you and
remain with you for ever. Amen.[2]

9
Ciaran of Clonmacnoise

We preach the Christ that was nailed to a cross.

1 Corinthians 1:23

PILGRIM TRAVELS

Monday, July 22
Kells and Clonmacnoise

We are in Ireland today heading south across the border with a first stop in Kells and the house where the Book of Kells was probably completed. Later in the day the sky clears and the sun shines over the river Shannon as I arrive at Clonmacnoise. A new information center welcomes the pilgrim visitor to this lovely setting. So many of these centers have been erected recently to accommodate the tourist industry. The great high crosses I view as I enter the grounds are impressive. Several budding archaeologists are working on diggings, loosening the turf, uncovering a gravestone, and then recovering the stone with the turf to protect it.

If I ever come to Clonmacnoise again, it will be by boat from Athlone along the lovely Shannon, the way most of the pilgrims first came.

The peaceful tranquility here invites contemplation. History, however, has been unkind to Clonmacnoise and other similar sacred sites for there is no longer an active, worshiping monastic community in residence. Holy Cross Abbey in Ireland is significant because it is perhaps the only ruined mission center in Ireland that has been reclaimed by the people for its original purposes, and that took a special act of government. During the occupation of Ireland by the British, the Anglican Church of Ireland became the custodian of the buildings, many of which were destroyed either during Henry VIII's reign or afterward. The agreement does not allow the buildings to be used by the Roman Catholic Church. As a result, today you will find a lovely tourist center housed in a beautiful sanctuary in Dublin.

Ciaran or Kieran of Clonmacnoise (c. 512-545)

Thirty-three years were all that Ciaran was given. He died of cholera shortly after founding the Clonmacnoise monastery. Standing here today in the quiet countryside admiring the view of the Shannon and listening to the birds, I find it difficult to picture this site as a great learning and artistic center on the crossroads of ancient Ireland. But indeed, along with Armagh, Kildare, Glendalough, and Iona, it was one of the great mission centers of its day.

Tradition tells us Ciaran's father was Boite, a carpenter who specialized in chariot making. His father had moved to Roscommon to avoid the high taxes and there Ciaran was born around 512 with a love of learning in his genes. His maternal grandfather was a bard, one of those ancient Celtic singing poets who composed and recited verses on the legends and history of their tribes. Finnian, who had studied at Ninian's Candida Casa in Whithorn, founded a school at Clonnard where Ciaran prepared for ministry. He continued his training with Enda, a mentor and soul friend, spending several years with him on Inis Mor or Inishmore in the windswept Aran Islands. Eventually Ciaran moved back to the mainland where he first established a mission center at Lough Ree on Hare Island and then later at Clonmacnoise. His many friends included Columba of Iona, students together; Finnian of Clonard; Enda of the Aran Islands; and Kevin of Glendalough, a brother abbot.

While with Enda on Aran, Ciaran had a vision of a great, fruitful tree growing beside a stream in the middle of Ireland. The tree protected all of Ireland and its fruit was carried off to distant shores. In Enda's interpretation of the vision, Ciaran was the tree and all of Ireland would find shelter under his leadership. Encouraged by the vision, Ciaran left the Aran Islands to found Clonmacnoise on the banks of the river Shannon around January 545.

People of faith have a heightened sense of place. Some believe, as did Ciaran, that a site could be a "thin place" with less of a barrier there between heaven and earth. Because of this belief, when a special site was discovered by a holy man such as Ciaran, other monks would soon gather there as well, in the hope that they might also connect with God. Ciaran predicted that those buried in the "blessed soil of

Clonmacnoise would pass through that door on the way to heaven." Less than a year after founding the monastery, Ciaran died on September 9, 545. He fought to stay alive until Kevin, the abbot at Glendalough, came. They talked for a while, shared the Lord's Supper, and then Ciaran slipped away through that thin wall to be with God.

Clonmacnoise or Cluain Mhic Nois

Clonmacnoise, in Irish "the meadow of the sons of Nos," eventually became a major mission center, training disciples in all aspects of the faith. There were numerous wattle and daub huts for the members of the community and a number of small churches scattered about the site. In the middle of it all stood the small cathedral. To its east is the oratory or Temple of Ciaran, a ninth-century church where he is probably buried along with the Kings of Connaught and Tara.

For five hundred years from 700 to 1200, Clonmacnoise was a noisy, busy, congested community where arts and literature had the highest priority. The scriptorium produced many decorated gospel books and psalters over the years but none have survived. A secular book, *The Book of the Dun Cow*, a collection of Celtic tales, did.

The monastery chose its abbots well, thus maintaining its high standards during the years of its active life. Under the protection of High King Flannthe a stone cathedral was built around 900 and a High Cross of Scriptures carved. In 1124 the round tower was completed.

An Irish king first plundered the monastery in 833, killing many and burning the land. The Vikings followed in 842, returning in 845 to burn it to the ground. The Irish continued to plunder and burn during the next 300 years until the Normans attacked in 1179 and reduced what was left of the more than one hundred buildings to ashes. The English troops carried off whatever they could lay their hands on in 1552. The center finally fell into ruin following the devastation by Cromwell's troops a hundred years later.

Clonmacnoise is strategically located at the crossroads of the beautiful Shannon, Ireland's longest river, which runs north and south, and a trail that runs east and west. Since 1955 Clonmacnoise has been protected as a national monument site which now houses some of the finest monastic ruins and high crosses in Ireland.

Closing Reflection:
High Crosses and Round Towers

The Celtic people were an oral people. They depended on the spoken rather than the written word. The Druids spent long years memorizing the history and the laws of the land in order to pass them on to the next generation. As more people turn to television for their entertainment and information, and less to the written word, they become more orally oriented. They are less skilled in writing and more oriented to communicating by phone rather than letters.

The Celts eventually learned how to write from the Romans. They developed a love of literacy and transcribed books almost night and day. In his book *How the Irish Saved Civilization*, Thomas Cahill argues that it is precisely in this way that they had the opportunity to save civilization. But their culture as a whole was still an oral culture. If you were unable to recall something, you simply did not know it. Let's explore how they communicated their faith.

Round Towers

The sixty-three-foot round tower at Clonmacnoise was built in 1124 of finely shaped limestone blocks. The tower entrance, a door eleven feet above the ground, faces the main west door of the cathedral church, thus allowing it to be seen by people leaving the sanctuary. The Irish word for round tower, *cloigtheach*, means belfry, but the bells rung here would have been handbells to call the people to prayer.

Round towers had many functions; scholars can only guess at what they were. They may have been landmarks for the pilgrims walking toward them from a distance; bell towers calling the monks to prayer; watchtowers for spotting Viking raiders; storehouses for Bibles, books, and relics; or places of refuge in times of attack. Some believe that the pilgrims would gather around the tower where a monk in the high entrance could display the relics they came to revere high above the heads of the crowds.

The High Crosses

The high crosses were preaching stations where pilgrims would gather to hear the stories depicted on the cross. The sandstone shafts of these high crosses were usually carved with a combination of swirling Celtic designs and scenes from the Bible. These high crosses created visual images designed to remind the viewer of a biblical story. For the pilgrim it was a focus of meditation; for the searcher it was a way of learning; for the speaker it was an illustration for their story.

At the center of the cross was Jesus. One side would depict him arms outstretched on a cross, the other side the risen Jesus at the last judgment. The ring around the center probably represented either the world or the sun. The importance of baptism was recognized by scenes from the life of John the Baptist. Some crosses carried images of the desert hermits, Paul and Anthony, as a tribute to the monastic life. Images were often carved on all four sides of the cross. Since the three high crosses at Clonmacnoise are among the artistic treasures of Ireland, they have been replaced by excellent cast replicas and the originals are now protected from the climate inside the visitors' center.

The high crosses and round towers enabled the Celtic Christians to proclaim the message of God's love. How do we communicate within an oral culture today? Some suggestions include sermons that are more story-oriented, posters with thought-provoking sayings, buttons and banners that raise awareness and provoke questions, and small groups in which relationships are developed and life stories shared.

Faith Sharing: The Good News

For Christ did not send me to baptize but to proclaim the gospel, and not with eloquent wisdom, so that the cross of Christ might not be emptied of its power. For the message about the cross is foolishness to those who are perishing, but to us who are being saved it is the power of God. For it is written, "I will destroy the wisdom of the wise, and the discernment of the discerning I will thwart." Where is the one who is wise? Where is the scribe? Where is the debater of this age? Has not God made foolish the wisdom of the world? For since, in the wisdom of God, the world did not know God through wisdom, God decided, through the foolishness of our proclamation, to save those who believe.

For Jews demand signs and Greeks desire wisdom, but we proclaim Christ crucified, a stumbling block to Jews and foolishness to Gentiles, When I came to you, brothers and sisters, I did not come proclaiming the mystery of God to you in lofty words or wisdom. For I decided to know nothing among you except Jesus Christ, and him crucified. And I came to you in weakness and in fear and in much trembling. My speech and my proclamation were not with plausible words of wisdom, but with a demonstration of the Spirit and of power, so that your faith might rest not on human wisdom but on the power of God. Yet among the mature we do speak wisdom, though it is not a wisdom of this age or of the rulers of this age, who are doomed to perish. (1 Corinthians 1:17–23, 2:1–6)

The story that Christianity had to tell did not make sense either to the pious Jew or the cultured Greek. Paul quotes Isaiah's prediction that this would happen, that wisdom would fail. As an example he cites the fact that for all its wisdom, most of the world has never found and is still seeking God. The cross was a stumbling block for the Jews for they could not conceive of a suffering messiah; rather, they looked to a messiah in the tradition of David, someone who would produce something spectacular. The message of the cross was nonsense to the Greeks. They believed God would never come in human form. The good news was also too blunt and unsophisticated for them, lacking the fine words and wisdom of philosophical debate. How then are we to communicate the gospel? Tell it simply and truthfully, from the heart.

Personal Reflection

1. Stained glass windows and high crosses were developed to tell the story of Christian faith. What are some ways that we can tell the story of God's love in an oral and visual society?

Closing Prayer

The Cross of Christ
upon your brow.
The Cross of Christ
protect you now.

The Cross of Christ
upon your mind.
The Cross of Christ
make you kind.

The Cross of Christ
upon your head.
The Cross of Christ
save from dread.

The Cross of Christ
upon your face.
The Cross of Christ
give you grace.
The Cross of Christ
upon your heart.
The Cross of Christ
set you apart.
The Cross of Christ
upon your soul.
The Cross of Christ
keep you whole.[1]

10
Kevin of Glendalough

Keep on being faithful to what you were taught and to what you believed.

2 Timothy 3:14

PILGRIM TRAVELS

Thursday, July 18

Unlike the rainy day when I was first here, people are all over the place. The new visitors' center is a welcome oasis staffed by gracious people. There has been a huge investment in upgrading the tourist scene with money and visitors coming from the European community. Our guide allows us to enter Kevin's eleventh-century chapel, an early Irish oratory or preaching place with a steep roof of overlapping stones, a small round window, and a round tower belfry. Although the original timber floor is missing, the walls and roof after all these years remain as a witness to its mission.

The grounds are pleasant and extensive. Great for hiking!

Kevin or Cóemhghein (498-618)

Kevin or Cóemhghein, meaning "fair begotten," was a hermit living in solitude in the beautiful wilderness area of Glendalough when God called him to form a mission center that became one of the largest communities in Ireland. Born into one of the ruling families in Leinster, Kevin received an education from three monks, Eoghan, Lochan, and Éanna. Then he retreated to the quiet valley of Glendalough where he made his hermit's home near the upper lake in a cave, possibly recycling a Bronze-Age tomb.

Attracted by his piety and wisdom, monks gradually gathered around him, forming a small community which soon became a monastery. The community grew and then relocated down near the lower lake. In 570 Kevin was asked officially to be its spiritual leader or abbot. "Abbot" (from "Abba," as in the Lord's Prayer) means father. Thousands of students flocked here from all over Ireland, Britain, and Europe. Late in life, Kevin became a hermit once again seeking solitude by the upper lake. By the time he died, the foundation at Glendalough had been laid for several hundred years of ministry and mission as an attractive learning center.

Glendalough

The monastic ruins of Gleann-da-Locha or Glen of the Two Lakes lie twenty-five miles south of Dublin in a valley between two clear water lakes. A surprising number of buildings remain despite the many attacks by Irish raiders and Danish Vikings in the ninth and tenth centuries. Besides being an important historical site in Ireland, Glendalough is one of the more attractive with the pine and spruce of the Wicklow mountains providing a gorgeous backdrop.

Although the monastery was revived in the twelfth century, English forces destroyed it during the summer of 1398. Major restoration was begun in 1875, and today there is an excellent interpretation center with a cordial crew that welcomes everyone with an audiovisual orientation tracing the monastic history of Ireland written by noted author and historian, Peter Harbison.

The grounds, as at all the monastic sites I visited, are somewhat misleading since only the ruined stone buildings remain. At the height of their activity, there would have been many wooden dwellings, workshops, areas for copying manuscripts, guest houses, a hospital, and farm buildings.

The first settlement by the Upper Lake had its focus in the little "Church of the Rock," or Teampull na Skellig, which is located in the lake and can only be reached by boat. Kevin's cell, approximately ten feet in diameter, overlooks the lake. Along the lower lake are the ruins of the later monastic site. The grounds are entered through a unique gateway, the only example of its kind in Ireland, which still has two fine granite arches although its timber roof is long gone. The twelfth-century cathedral is the largest building on the site with a chancel and a nave that was forty-five by thirty feet. Kevin's twelve-foot cross stands nearby, one of the four crosses that were stations on the pilgrim way.

The well-maintained round tower, more than 100 feet high, was built of mica-slate and granite in the eleventh or twelfth centuries, probably in response to the number of pilgrims that visited the area. Its entrance, twelve feet above ground, would be perfect for a monk to display the artifacts that would attract the pilgrim and to lead services for a crowd. The six stories each had a timber floor connected by ladders with four windows at the fourth floor level and four at the top.

Closing Reflection: Scribal Scholars

Some of the best minds of that period came from far and near to Glendalough to learn. The monks explored as many branches of the tree of knowledge as they could climb. From dawn to dusk they copied, not only the gospels and the early church sermons and commentaries, but also the old Irish tales and any literature available. Challenged by the tales they read from the Bible and the histories of the early Christian martyrs, they wondered how they could follow in the steps of those who had given so much for their faith.

During the time of Patrick and later of Kevin, the monks found an answer. This came to be called the Green Martyrdom, as opposed to the bloody Red Martyrdom of the Roman arenas. Green martyrs retreated to mountaintops, deserts, or lonely islands such as Mount Skellig, leaving behind the comforts and pleasures you and I enjoy, to study the Scriptures and talk with God.

Ninian knew of the green martyrs, those monks such as Anthony who wrestled with God as hermits in the desert. Anthony was so revered he appears on some of their high crosses. Kevin was greatly influenced by the concept of Green Martyrdom, and he practiced it as a hermit at Glendalough. When others came seeking wisdom and faith from this holy man who had wrestled with God in the wilderness, a monastery was formed around him as it had around Anthony. Centers such as Glendalough grew into villages and small towns, becoming centers of learning, of business, and of the creative arts. Hospitality was a Celtic trait and no one was turned away.

The centers gathered texts from all over, copying them and storing them in their libraries. As Rome fell and Europe descended into the superstitious Dark Ages where few could read or write, these centers became a reservoir of written resources.

At this time occurred what came to be called White Martyrdom. Brave men and women sailed from the land they loved, never to return, to share the good news with those in foreign lands. For instance, Columba left behind his beloved Ireland—worse than dying, he said—and sailed for Iona to share the good news with the Picts. When the number of monks at Iona reached 150, Columba organized a group, a leader and twelve monks, and sent them out to establish their own mission center. His monks took with them the monastic life-style—to farm, pray, study, and copy—and the monastic organizational style, a hut for each monk, a slightly bigger one for the abbot, and a guest house for the visitors. When Columba died, sixty centers had been established.

Columbanus, one of these traveling Irish monks, left with twelve others in 590, when he was fifty, to form a mission center in Gaul. He soon established three and just as quickly clashed with the bishops and other clergy in the area whom he accused of being not aggressive enough in winning converts for Christ. They deported him. He was saved along with some of his companions when the ship sank. Eventually they wandered into Bobbio where they built the first Irish-Italian monastery.

And so the cycle becomes complete. Literate Romans educated the people of Britain, who then taught the Irish, who returned to the continent to educate the illiterate Europeans. Thomas Cahill writes, "The White Martyrs, clothed like druids in distinctive white wool robes, fanned out cheerfully across Europe, founding monasteries that would become famous cities…. Wherever they went, the Irish brought with them their books…their love of learning and their skills at bookmaking."[1]

What was it like to be a scribal scholar spending your waking hours creating texts for preservation and study? Sandwiched between some lines in a manuscript was a poetic side-note jotted there by some imaginative scholar comparing his work with the work of his cat, Pangur Ban. The monk hunted words while the cat hunted mice; they both had skills that brought satisfaction. His jottings were translated by Robin Flowers in the form of a delightful poem (*The Irish Tradition*, 1947, Oxford University Press).

Monks gathered in the monastery's cloister area during daylight to copy texts which were stored in their libraries. Often a senior monk read from a text while the other monks copied what was dictated. Manuscripts often took years to produce because monks not only attended chapel, often up to eight times a day, but also took turns in the kitchen and garden.

The manuscripts were written on quality vellum or parchment

(animal skins). Skins were prepared by soaking in lime to dissolve the hair, stretched, scraped clean, and then trimmed and sewn together. The Lindisfarne gospels were written on 130 sheets and the Book of Kells on 185. Unlike their counterparts on the continent, Celtic scribes used the suede side which reacted better with their ink and colors. Manuscripts often were illuminated. The portrait of St. Matthew found in the Book of Durrow is the oldest Celtic art portrait we have.

Faith Sharing: Paul's Instructions to Timothy

Now you have observed my teaching, my conduct, my aim in life, my faith, my patience, my love, my steadfastness, my persecutions and suffering the things that happened to me in Antioch, Iconium, and Lystra. What persecutions I endured! Yet the Lord rescued me from all of them. Indeed, all who want to live a godly life in Christ Jesus will be persecuted. But wicked people and impostors will go from bad to worse, deceiving others and being deceived.

But as for you, continue in what you have learned and firmly believed, knowing from whom you learned it, and how from childhood you have known the sacred writings that are able to instruct you for salvation through faith in Christ Jesus. All scripture is inspired by God and is useful for teaching, for reproof, for correction, and for training in righteousness, so that everyone who belongs to God may be proficient, equipped for every good work.

In the presence of God and of Christ Jesus, who is to judge the living and the dead, and in view of his appearing and his kingdom, I solemnly urge you: proclaim the message; be persistent whether the time is favorable or unfavorable; convince, rebuke, and encourage, with the utmost patience in teaching. For the time is coming when people will not put up with sound doctrine, but having itching ears, they will accumulate for themselves teachers to suit their own desires, and will turn away from listening to the truth and wander away to myths. As for you, always be sober, endure suffering, do the work of an evangelist, carry out your ministry fully. (2 Timothy 3:10—4:5)

This letter, written as if by an older, experienced pastor, Paul, to a younger pastor, Timothy, gives advice on what to expect in the years of ministry that lay ahead. Paul was not naive about the difficulties the next generation of believers would face. He knew pastors would be challenged severely. He knew the next generation of believers could be confused and tempted away from the faith. Two thousand years later it is still happening.

How will Christians be able to find their way through these

challenging times? Paul suggests at least four answers that hold true even today. You can find your way through confusing times by:

1. Being faithful to what you were taught and to what you believed;
2. remembering who taught you these things;
3. recalling the Holy Scriptures that you have known since childhood; and
4. having faith in Christ Jesus.

We are living in a time marked by confusion and change. Paul's advice is still good. He doesn't promise us comfort or an easy way; but whatever else may be said of this life of ministry that we share, it certainly won't be dull!

Personal Reflection

1. Since the Bible is so important to Christian living, what are you doing to make it a guide for your life? Do you have a favorite translation you use for reading Scripture? Why?

Closing Prayer

May the words we write be inspired by God.
May the words we say come from Jesus.
May the words we believe become alive in us
by the power of the Spirit.
May the Trinity flow through our words
and our lives, now and forever. Amen.

11

Columba
and Iona

The followers in Antioch decided to send whatever help they could to Judea.

Acts 11:29

PILGRIM TRAVELS

Monday, July 1
Hartford to Heathrow

My express flight to New York is cancelled. The good news is that, since I won't be seeing my wife for five weeks, we have time for a relaxed supper together at the Sheraton before catching the next flight. The bad news is that I will be a half day late in arriving on Iona. This reminds me of the advice I give all travelers: "Travel necessitates being a good-natured realist, as well as a romantic, and requires an agreeable acceptance of situations as they exist; not as each of us might prefer them to be. A pleasant tolerance makes for an enjoyable travel experience."

Tuesday, July 2
Heathrow to Oban

Arriving in Glasgow ahead of my luggage but way behind schedule, I head for the Tourist Information Center to reserve a place to stay in Oban for the night knowing I won't make Iona nor my room there as planned. The evening train, the Highlander, flows along the banks of the River Clyde up to Oban. Once out of the urban area, it becomes a pretty ride with beautiful purple flowers and mystic castles marking the way. The town is dark and deserted when I arrive. Tossing my travel bag over my shoulder, I walk out into the light rain to find my room for the night. My sport jacket begins to feel damp by the time I locate my host for the evening. After calling home to let everyone know I have arrived safely, although minus my suitcase, the warm, dry bed welcomes me. My pilgrimage has begun!

Wednesday, July 3
Oban to Iona

With a great Scottish breakfast under my belt, I am ready to face the world. Oh to be in Scotland in July! Knowing protection will be needed from the elements on Iona, I buy a light, rainproof jacket in a hiking shop on the way to the ferry. Oban is a small fishing town with a typical British waterfront area. The town rises to a high hill on which is built a folly, a Roman Coliseum, constructed by a banker to create work for the town at the turn of the century.

The ferry waiting room is filled with the sounds of Pentecost, the many languages of pilgrims headed for Iona. A cup of hot chocolate and a scone make the thirty-minute crossing to the Island of Mull pass quickly. The thirty-seven-mile bus ride across the island provides great shots for my camera. The mountains with their icy cold streams flashing white as they flow over the scattered rocks live up to the expectations created by calendar pictures of Scotland. Several white owls fly near the coach as we drive by. The Fionphort ferry to Iona is a challenge; steep ramps down and then up. It is a good thing I don't have my suitcase after all. God does work in mysterious ways.

Iona is all I hoped it would be—isolated, mountainous, rocky, and desolate. On arriving here in 1773, Samuel Johnson commented that his piety grew warmer among the ruins of Iona. May it be so for me and for all pilgrims who arrive here.

After lunching at the Heritage Center, I immerse myself in the island's sites including the abbey. Its bookstore contains a variety of Celtic books including those written by members of the Iona community. Sheep are all around. Supper at Clachancorrach, the small farm where I am staying, is delicious. When Batman appears on the living room TV, I head for bed, happy to be here.

Thursday, July 4

An American flag is hanging in the coffee shop today to celebrate our Independence Day. A quick call to the airport in Glasgow reveals that my luggage has arrived. I ask them to hold it and I will pick it up tomorrow.

As I wander around the abbey, I hear the choir rehearsing for this evening's service. Lunch is again at the Heritage Center, where I meet Susan, a summer volunteer. After worship at the parish kirk, I sit briefly in the abbey peace garden until it begins to rain and then enter the abbey for the afternoon worship service for day visitors, which today is based on the theme of peace and justice. This service is for the thousands who come each year for day visits, arriving in the morning and leaving later in the afternoon. To really appreciate the island, however, you need to spend at least a night or two.

After reading for a while, I walk over to Dun Craig or "brown cow," a Christian ecumenical quiet house. Jenny, the head resident, treats me to a cup of coffee and fruitcake and we chat. After enjoying a few quiet moments reading in the living room, Jenny gives me a lift to the restaurant. Evening worship follows dinner, and the combination of words and song around the theme of commitment touches me deeply. My journey begins to seem like a pilgrimage rather than a tour. During the coffee hour afterward Susan introduces me to the library which is filled with Celtic books, although most are dated. Then she completes the tour by driving me around the tiny island pointing out the restaurant, two hotels, the schoolhouse which has four students, the grocery store and gift shop, the two farms and ten crofts (small family-owned farms). It is cold and windy.

The people and the worship, three times on Thursday, make the Iona experience all worth the effort. This certainly is a "thin place" where there are few distractions and where there is an atmosphere that encourages a deeper relationship with God.

Columba or Columcille (521-597)

Although Columba could have been a king, he chose the life of a monk and evangelist. Born on December 7, 521 at Garten, in Donegal, Northern Ireland of royal parents, he was educated both in druidic lore by Gemman, a bard, and the Christian faith by Finnian. Outside of Ireland he was known as Columba, but his name as a monk in Ireland was Columcille (pronounced koll-m-kill), which means "dove of the church." Influenced by Martin of Tours as Ninian had been, Columba became a tireless evangelist, founding a number of churches in Ireland and several monasteries including those at Derry in 546, Durrow in 556, Kells, and the Iona mission in Scotland in 563.

In 561 at the age of forty-two, Columba, seeking new challenges and a change of surroundings, sailed from the coast of Derry with twelve companions in a *curragh*, a seagoing coracle or boat made of leather hide over wood. His biographer, Adamnan, tells us he quit the shores of Ireland to become a *peregrinus*, a wanderer or pilgrim for Jesus.

One tale tells why he left Ireland for the rigors of Iona. Columba had a deep love of books, especially beautifully designed and bound manuscripts. As a student he fell in love with Finnian's uniquely decorated book of psalms and secretly made a copy by working after hours each night. Caught in the act, he was hauled before Diarmait, King of Ireland, who issued what must have been one of the first copyright decrees, "To every cow her calf; to every book its copy." Columba turned over the copy to Finnian but kept a grudge against the king. Payback time came when, under orders from Diarmait, one of Columba's followers was killed. God, Columba claimed, must be avenged. Calling the northern O'Neill clan together, they defeated Diarmait, a southern O'Neill, at Cuildremhue in 561 with the loss of many lives. Because he had broken his vows as a monk not to take up arms, he was exiled from his beloved Ireland and ordered to save as many souls as had died in battle. This is a good tale but probably not true. Columba was more likely inspired to spread the gospel to those who had not been reached. The record indicates he returned several times to Ireland so it is unlikely his missionary work was a punishment.

In 563 Columba obtained permission from Brude, the Pict king, to establish a monastery on the tiny island of Iona, a former Druid sanctuary. On May 12 he landed with twelve followers at Port-a-Curach. It is said the first thing he did on arriving at Iona was to climb to its highest hill and search the horizon for the Irish shores. Satisfied that he could not be tempted by their sight to return, he stayed. The hill is known as Carn Cul Ri Eirinn or the Hill of the Turning Back to Ireland. Just as Patrick left Britain for a mission in Ireland, Columba left his native land to witness to those who had never heard of Jesus. For thiry-five years he worked to bring God's peace to the Picts.

In the years ahead Iona would become one of the greatest Celtic centers for mission, learning, and culture. The monastery rapidly grew to house 150 monks, a number they would maintain by organizing mission parties of twelve monks and a leader to establish new mission centers. From Iona came the missionaries who effectively evangelized most of Scotland and northern Britain. Their influence extended throughout Europe.

These missionaries tailored their approach to the culture around them. They targeted the kings and princes who, if converted, would then allow them to minister in their area. Columba, as abbot of Iona, was tribal chieftain of his village, a political diplomat mediating treaties with opposing kings, and a pious monk leading his followers closer to God. He claimed Pict territory as his mission even to the point of discouraging the Whithorn monks from establishing mission centers there.

There were three classes of monks: the older or senior monks who led the worship services and copied the texts; the monks who farmed; and the students who came from all over Europe. Columba taught his monks on Iona to show hospitality not only to these human visitors but also to the birds who flew to the island.

The last day of his life, June 9, 597, found Columba copying Psalm 34. He stopped at the tenth verse, "Those who seek the Lord lack no good thing." That night when the monks arose for the midnight service, Columba joined them, blessed them, and died.

Columba foresaw the day when his monks would leave the island and the buildings would lie in ruins. His prophecy, made more than one thousand years ago, may be coming true today.

"Iona of my heart, Iona of my love, instead of monk's voices shall be lowing of cattle;/ But ere the world end, Iona will be as it was."

Iona

The Hebrides or Western Isles of Scotland consist of more than fifty islands; Iona is one of them. This tiny jewel has rock, heather, moor, meadows, and a population of 100 on an island of 2,000 acres that is 3.5 miles long and 1.5 miles wide. It is separated from the southern tip of Mull by a short strip of water easily crossed by a ferry today. Originally used by the Druids who believed the island was a "thin place," the island was chosen as a mission site by Columba. It is possible that an earlier Christian settlement of Patrick's followers may have preceded Columba. The Iona mission was a typical Celtic village of simple huts in a circle around a central green. The movement grew in influence as it sponsored other mission centers. Columba crowned Aidan King of Scots at Iona on the Destiny Stone, which could be the famous Stone of Scone. Iona's fourteen-foot high St. Martin's cross, built in the eighth century, is complete and original.

In 802 the Vikings raided the mission, slaughtering sixty-eight monks on the sands of "martyrs bay." The few monks who remained retreated to Dunkeld, the new center of the Columban mission, or to Ireland. The Book of Kells, now on view at the Trinity College library, almost certainly was produced on Iona in the late eighth or ninth centuries and then taken to Kells, also a Columban mission, where it was finished. Thought to be the work of many hands, it is estimated that 150 calves must have been needed for its vellum pages. Its 340 surviving pages all have vivid color illustrations which seem to be influenced by Egyptian art, reinforcing the connection between the Egyptian influence of Anthony of the Desert and Celtic missions. Illustrations in the book include the distinctive Celtic knot and a butterfly escaping from a cocoon, a symbol of the resurrection.

Bridging the pagan and Christian heritage at Iona is the ancient burial site, Reilig Odhráin, where kings from Scotland, Ireland, France, and Norway are buried. Macbeth and his wife, Gruach, were buried here in 1058. In 1203 a group of Benedictine monks came to Iona and built the Norman Abbey which still stands today. A convent was founded about the same time and its ruins are still present. Although the island was home once again to a monastic mission, its character had radically changed from the huts which had housed Columba's followers.

Iona's call from the past today attracts thousands to this speck of rock, so isolated from the rest of the world, those who come to walk, rest, pray, and rededicate themselves to do mission and ministry in a meaningful way.

Closing Reflection: The Iona Community

Today Iona is home to a restored Celtic mission. When the depression of the thirties hit hard, George MacLeod, a young Presbyterian pastor, reached out to his community, Glasgow, drawing hundreds into his congregation. His dream of training others for an urban ministry found a home at Iona where the abbey had become part of the Church of Scotland. Of Iona he writes, it is a "thin place with only a tissue paper separating earth from heaven." In 1938 craftsmen and pastors began the job of rebuilding. Although lumber was scarce during the war years, one stormy night a Canadian ship dumped its timber cargo which landed on Mull opposite Iona.

Influenced by the great themes of Celtic Christianity, George MacLeod sought to make the Iona community a living force in our time. The Celtic symbol of intertwining the secular and sacred, material and spiritual, endlessly moving and returning to where it started, is a symbol of his life and ministry. Although it remains a place of pilgrimage, attracting more than 150,000 people each summer, the Abbey community is an extension of the Glasgow city mission which continues Columba's emphasis on caring for a deeply troubled world. Although people come to Iona to draw closer to God, they also learn to pray about environmental concerns, commitment to peace and justice, ministering to the poor, and developing interfaith dialogue. Although basically a Scottish community, it has members throughout the world who keep in touch through their newsletter, *The Coracle*. They publish worship materials under the Wild Goose name, the Celtic symbol for Spirit. "God has renewed his island—and now he is renewing us." (George MacLeod)

Faith Sharing: The Church in Antioch

Now those who were scattered because of the persecution that took place over Stephen traveled as far as Phoenicia, Cyprus, and Antioch, and they spoke the word to no one except Jews. But among them were some men of Cyprus and Cyrene who, on coming to Antioch, spoke to the Hellenists also, proclaiming the Lord Jesus. The hand of the Lord was with them, and a great number became believers and turned to the Lord.

News of this came to the ears of the church in Jerusalem, and they sent Barnabas to Antioch. When he came and saw the grace of God, he rejoiced, and he exhorted them all to remain faithful to the Lord with steadfast devotion; for he was a good man, full of the Holy Spirit and of faith. And a great many people were brought to the Lord.

Then Barnabas went to Tarsus to look for Saul, and when he had found him, he brought him to Antioch. So it was that for an entire year they met with the church and taught a great many people, and it was in Antioch that the disciples were first called "Christians." At that time prophets came down from Jerusalem to Antioch. One of them named Agabus stood up and predicted by the Spirit that there would be a severe famine over all the world; and this took place during the reign of Claudius. The disciples determined that according to their ability, each would send relief to the believers living in Judea; this they did, sending it to the elders by Barnabas and Saul. (Acts of the Apostles 11:19–30)

The church in Antioch became a mission center for the thrust into the Roman Empire as Iona was to be for Scotland and England. After Stephen's death, believers scattered. As a result, Christian communities were soon in Ptolemais, Tyre, and Sidon. From these ports Christians sailed to Antioch in Syria, population 800,000, which was the capital and military center of the Roman province. The Romans remade the city in their image improving the road system and the port. Only Rome outshone it as a city. Communication was rapid, a fact that helped the witnessing church. At first preaching was aimed toward the Jews, but in this city of mixed race and culture, many searching Greeks had become "God-fearers," drawn to God and worshiping in the synagogue. When the Christians separated from the synagogue, many of these Greeks followed.

The Jerusalem church sent Barnabas, a Cypriot, to establish a relationship with the church at Antioch. He came, affirmed what they were doing, and became a leader in the church. Growth was such that Barnabas soon felt the need of an assistant. He remembered Paul, who for some years now had been going from place to place in Syria preaching the faith he had tried to destroy. After a long search he found his man and they returned together to Antioch where for a year they worked together. At that time the congregation decided to sponsor them on what was to become "the first missionary journey." The people of Antioch were the first to call the followers of the Way "Christians." It was meant to be a derogatory term, meaning "Christ lovers or followers."

Personal Reflection

1. People come to Iona to draw closer to God. They also learn to pray about environmental concerns, commitment to peace and justice, ministering to the poor, and developing interfaith dialogue. What are you doing or could do in one of those areas?

Closing Prayer

*We feel loved as members
of the family of God.
We know peace as brothers and sisters
walking with Jesus.
We sense the inspiration of the Spirit
in our lives, blessing us.
We are the people of the Way
who are known as Christians.*

12

Aidan and Lindisfarne

When Jesus had finished praying, one of his disciples said to him,
"Lord, teach us to pray."

Luke 11:1

PILGRIM TRAVELS

Saturday, July 6

The tide will cover the causeway in the evening so I time my arrival to cross in the late afternoon. Marygate House, a Christian retreat center, is where I will hang my hat tonight. Most of the visitors to the island come and go during the day leaving it at peace at night. After evensong I join the rest of the community for dinner.

While taking pictures of this lovely island after supper, I meet David Adam, noted Celtic scholar and writer. He serves as the Anglican priest of the parish church and is on his way to close the church doors for the night. We chat about books and things Celtic as the sun sets over the water. It is a pleasure to remain on the island and wander meditatively around the site. The evening closes with a good book in Marygate's library which, as you might guess, has a good selection of Celtic books.

Sunday, July 7

Since I can't leave the island until the tide goes out, I sleep in this morning. On the way to worship at the parish church, I buy David Adam's book. He poses for a picture with me and then signs his book *Border Lands* with this blessing, "The good and gracious God grant you a glimpse of glory." The tide is down now, so it's time to leave.

Aidan

A beautiful statue of Aidan stands today near the ruins of the Lindisfarne abbey showing him holding the torch of faith he brought to the Angles. Bishop Lightfoot of Durham hailed him as "The Apostle of England." This Celtic monk, bishop, and missionary combined worship, work, and witness in his ministry. The image of Jesus was reflected in this gentle and humble man. Aidan came from Ireland to live at Iona where he heard the call to share the faith with the people of northeastern England.

When Oswald, who had studied at Iona, returned to northeastern England in 633 to lead an uprising against Penda, a pagan king, their armies clashed at Hadrian's Wall at Heavenfield near Hexham. Inspired by the high crosses of Iona, Oswald erected one of wood before which the troops gathered and prayed. Although outnumbered, they won, establishing a base at Bamburgh. Oswald desired to share the Christian faith with his people, and so he turned to the monks of Iona. Corman arrived only to return, complaining that he could make no headway with these "obstinate, barbarous" Angles. When the order met to assess the situation, Aidan suggested a little patience. "You could have been a little bit gentler, brother." The order decided Aidan was the gentle man for the job, appointed him a bishop, and sent him in 635 with twelve other monks to England.

Aidan requested Lindisfarne or Holy Island for his mission center, an island where the tides flood the connecting land twice a day. Here he established his mission within view of Oswald's residence at Bamburgh on the mainland. When he needed solitude, Aidan retreated to a hermitage on the Farne Islands six miles out.

At first Oswald traveled with Aidan, acting as translator and sharing in the work. Later, after he learned the language, Aidan traveled on foot alone in order to maintain close contact with the people, especially the poor and the stranger. Oswald's reputation spread as a king who was just and caring, but he was not destined to live long. Nine years after becoming king, Oswald was killed in a rematch with Penda.

The mission at Lindisfarne, however, survived and flourished. During Aidan's lifetime Christian communities were planted across northern England and in Scotland. One of these mission outposts was Melrose. Their discipline of self-denial included poverty, little sleep, and a spare diet. For those who came, the reward was access to some of the best teachers and education of their day, drawn from a mix of Druid and Christian teachings. Among the many lives Aidan influenced were those of Cuthbert, Bishop of Lindisfarne in 685, and

Hilda of Whitby. Lindisfarne was to become the mission center for bringing the Christian faith to the people of the north. The Lindisfarne Gospels, similar to the Book of Kells, came from here.

In 651, sixteen years after launching Lindisfarne, Aidan died and was buried on the island. The mission lasted for almost 250 years before being destroyed by the Vikings.

Lindisfarne or Holy Island

Lindisfarne or Holy Island, an island the size of Iona, lies off the coast of northeastern England. Tourists flock over the three-mile causeway which links Lindisfarne with the mainland to visit the village, the ruined priory, and the castle. Rare birds, blown here by the storms, and all kinds of wildlife find sanctuary here.

The Vikings attacked in 793 destroying the buildings and killing many of the monks. The center continued but, after it was attacked again, the monks left in 875 not to return for more than 200 years. In 1082 the Benedictines established a cell on the island and people have been living here ever since. The priory was rebuilt in 1120 and named in honor of Cuthbert, a former abbot. Lindisfarne remained at peace for the next 400 years avoiding the raids of Vikings and Scots.

When King Henry VIII ruthlessly dissolved the monasteries, God's house on Lindisfarne was turned into an army camp and a castle was built from its stone. The Earl of Dunbar took the lead from the roof, the bells, and anything else of value aboard his ship which then sank along with all its stolen materials and many of the crew in what was credited as an act of God.

Closing Reflection: Prayer

At the turn of the century, Alexander Carmichael collected Celtic poems, prayers, and blessings from the Scottish Highlands in the classic six volumes of the *Carmina Gadelica*. These prayers hold in tension the cross and the world just as the high crosses do. Esther De Waal has selected and edited some in her books. She writes of how these prayers are incorporated in the daily habits of life:

> A woman kneels on the earth floor in her small hut in the Outer
> Hebrides and lights her fire with this prayer:

"I will kindle my fire this morning in the presence of the holy angels of heaven."

And as she banks the fire in the evening:
"As I save this fire tonight even so may Christ save me."[1]

Celtic Christians view prayer as talking with a friend. They see in creation the goodness and love of God. When we discover this, we have taken the first step in our prayer life—we know to whom we pray. The conversation we have with a loving God is what we call prayer.

We may begin by saying, "Gracious God, here is what I would like to tell you." Then we share what is on our hearts, minds, and souls. After this we pause and ask "What do you have to say to me?" Then in contemplation we quietly wait for an answer.

Here are some guidelines for prayer:

When. Jesus often prayed at the beginning or end of the day. Although we can obviously pray at anytime of the day, we should set a regular time for prayer and meditation.

Where. Jesus usually found a place apart in which to pray. He actually recommended a closet, that is, a place of privacy. We should adopt a place apart.

How. The position may be standing, sitting, kneeling, or lying down; we may pray in the manner that is most comfortable for us.

What. The words should be simple and direct, the way we naturally speak to a friend.

There is a pattern to prayer: praise, thanksgiving, confession, and requests for self and others. Based on this pattern, John Coburn lists these five foundation stones of prayer as responses to a loving God: "O God, I love you. I thank you for…(be specific). I am sorry for…(be specific). Please help (me)…help (Jane, John, etc.). Not my will, but yours be done."[2]

You can be certain that Jesus wants you to pray specifically for others and for yourself, and that he will answer those prayers in the best way which, of course, may not be the way we wish.

Faith Sharing: Teach Us to Pray

He was praying in a certain place, and after he had finished, one of his disciples said to him, "Lord, teach us to pray, as John taught his disciples." He said to them, "When you pray, say: Father, hallowed be your name. Your kingdom come. Give us each day our daily bread. And forgive us our sins, for we ourselves forgive everyone indebted to us. And do not bring us to the time of trial." (Luke 11:1–4)

Jesus prays and his prayer life now prompts a request from his disciples to teach them a community prayer that summarizes his teachings as other rabbis have done. In response he gives them a prayer they are to say together that includes five petitions.

They are encouraged to pray simply and directly to God as Abba or Father, and to expect that their Father will delight in answering their prayers, just as a loving human father does. They are to honor God's name in all that they do. They are to pray and work for the coming of God's kingdom on earth. They are to pray for daily food since they, the disciples, will be dependent on those who hear their witness to extend them hospitality. Just as they have daily need of bread, they also have an ongoing need for forgiveness. Here Luke uses "sinners" for his Greek readers; Matthew substitutes "debts" for his Jewish readers. And finally they are to pray that the pressure may not be so great that they cannot withstand it; an example would be Jesus in Gethsemane. Neither Matthew nor Luke includes the closing doxology used by many Christian denominations.

Personal Reflections

1. How do you typically pray? Do you have a set time? Place? Way of praying? Did you learn anything new from the above reflections on prayer? How will you put them into use?

Closing Prayer

Lord you are in this place,
Fill us with your power,
Cover us with your peace,
Show us your presence.
Lord help us to know,
We are in your hands,
We are under your protection,
We are covered by your love.
Lord we ask you today,
To deliver us from evil,
To guide us in our travels,
To defend us from all harm.
Lord give us now,
Eyes to see the invisible,
Ears to hear your call,
Hands to do your work,
And hearts to respond to your love.[3]

Better, though difficult, the right way to go,
Than wrong, though easy, where the end is woe.

13
Hilda
of Whitby

I am the way, the truth, and the life.

John 14:6

PILGRIM TRAVELS

Sunday, July 28

My pilgrimage comes to a close with a conference on "Celtic Spirituality and Modern Mission" at Durham. I have traveled the pilgrim path from Whithorn, where Ninian gave birth to a mission center, to Ireland and Iona and Lindisfarne. Those are the stages along the way that led to Whitby, where bishops, monks, and nuns debated the future of the church in England. This afternoon after worship in Durham Cathedral, I head for Whitby to stand where those who had argued in defense of the Celtic way had stood.

Nothing remains to be seen of Hilda's original Celtic monastery, Streoneshalh, which was destroyed by the Danish in 867. Even the name is gone, replaced by the Danish "Witebi" or Whitby. The Benedictine abbey, built in 1078, lies in ruins, closed in 1539. Although it has been at the mercy of the elements ever since, its fabulous windows and arches still remain a moving and graceful sight. Standing where the Celtic saints defended their tradition, I wonder if from these roots, there really could be a renewal of Celtic influence in the way we express our faith.

Children are climbing among the ruins. A storyteller recounts the saga of Caedmon, who was a lay brother at Whitby (c. 670), who is credited with writing the first English hymn by merging the Anglo-Saxon poetic song form with the words of the creation story.

The imposing ruins of the abbey are located high on a cliff above the town. As I drive toward the exit, the sun is setting over the River Esk and Whitby Bay, providing a spectacular view of this attractive mix of a medieval and a resort town. I click away with my camera, and then head for Durham. After four weeks on the road and more than 2,000 miles traveled, my pilgrimage is almost over. Only the resident conference at Durham remains.

Hilda or Hild (614-680)

Hilda founded the double monastery at Whitby that was to become the largest in England. She is another example of the way the Celts included women in leadership positions. Born a Northumbrian princess, she was baptized by Paulinus during his mission there. Arriving in 627, he left when the Christian king, Edwin, was killed in 633 by pagans. She remained true to her faith during the period that followed and, when Christian rule was reestablished, she set aside her royal heritage and became a nun.

After receiving training in a community in Gaul, Hilda was asked in 647 by Aidan, then bishop at Lindisfarne, to establish a mission center on the banks of the river Wear (pronounced "weir" as in "weird"). Her next challenge was as abbess at Hartlepool, where she wrote a Rule (a way of living) that governed the community's life. Celtic centers adopted their own Rule which allowed for some flexibility in the administration of their abbeys. Administration tended to be associational and horizontal—tasks shared by all and adapted to what was best for the local situation—rather than vertical, with a centralized authority who told everyone what to do.

Finally in 657 on land given her by King Oswy, she founded a double monastery for both monks and nuns at Streoneshalh or "the bay of the lighthouse," a name derived from the signal station the Romans had built there. The monastery became known for its scholarship, the gifted poet Caedmon, and for the Synod in 664 which was to decide the form of British Christianity until the Reformation. Hilda, although a strong adherent of the Celtic way, reluctantly conformed to the decision made by the king who had given her the land.

The historian Bede writes that all who knew her called her "mother," a form used by the desert Christians for women of wisdom. Her ministry emphasized justice, devotion, chastity, peace, and love. As many of the Celtic saints before her, Hilda had a love of birds who also loved her. It is said the wild geese stopped at Whitby to honor her as they made their seasonal flights. She died in the autumn of 680 after seven years of illness.

The Synod of Whitby (664)

The Celts kept the faith alive in Great Britain after the Roman army left in 410. Their centers at Whithorn, Iona, Lindisfarne, and Whitby planted Christianity so deeply it would never be uprooted again. But a challenge did come to the Celtic form of Christianity from Rome. In 597 Pope Gregory sent a missionary force, a party of Benedictine monks under Augustine, to the Angles in southern England. King Ethelbert, anxious to please his Christian queen, Bertha, agreed to grant land for a monastery at Canterbury in Kent. Augustine established a center there from which the form of the Christian faith shaped by Rome spread north. Gregory advised him that if he found things pleasing to God in the local ritual practices, he should adopt whatever would work to further the gospel. He seems to have ignored the pope's advice.

While the Celts, cut off during the Dark Ages from Europe, maintained the traditions they had learned, the Romans modified theirs. The two ways eventually clashed in the seventh century when Gregory was no longer around to advocate a more flexible approach. By now Rome was insisting on absolute authority and conformity, a request the Celtic communities resisted, preferring continuing autonomy and a relationship based on mutual respect. The differences eventually caused stress even in the royal family.

In Northumbria King Oswy's queen, who came from the south bringing her chaplain with her, celebrated the Easter of the Roman calendar while her husband held to the Celtic day of observance. Although both traditions celebrated Easter on Sunday, Rome had changed their minds in the fifth century about which Sunday and the Celts, isolated from Rome, remained true to the original date. Celtic monks also differed from their Roman counterparts by their tonsure or cut of their hair. The Romans shaved their heads on top, leaving a rim of hair around the ears, originally the mark of a Roman slave, and the Celts cut theirs shaved in front and long in the back. The abbot rather than the bishop was often the preeminent figure in the Celtic way. There were also differences in the practice of baptism, Mass, and ordination. Marriage was allowed for clergy, which the Welsh certainly practiced into the twelfth century.

In 664 the Celtic and Roman mission parties were called to meet at

Streoneshalh by King Oswy to resolve their differences. The King argued that if you serve one God, there should be one rule of life, and, as head of state, he would decide which was the truer form and then order his people to follow it in common. The church in Rome, empowered by the Roman emperor, had begun establishing an ecclesiastical empire which held that conformity was necessary in order to form a powerful organization. Thus, the basic issue became subservience to Rome, where the patterns of worship and service in the local church would be determined for all Christians. On the other hand, the Celtic tradition placed that power with the local congregation or mission center. Although both sides considered themselves part of the universal church, they expressed the issue of authority in different ways.

Bede, in his history of the English church, records the clash at Whitby. In one corner was Colman, a great missionary from Iona and now Bishop of Lindisfarne (661-664), who defended the Celtic observances, especially the date for Easter. He affirmed the way they dated Easter was practiced by his elders, listing Columba, Aidan, and other Celtic fathers, and by the disciple, John the Evangelist. In the other corner was wily Wilfred, an ambitious bishop with powerful connections in Rome, who affirmed the current Roman church law. He argued that whatever was practiced in Rome where Peter (holder of the "keys of the kingdom") and Paul lived, taught, suffered, and were buried, should be universal and, as such, Rome had the right to determine any practices. He argued that the Celts were opposing what the whole world was doing and demanded they recognize the authority of Rome rather than the guidance of God's Spirit.

In the end the king, keen to introduce some harmony into his kingdom, seemed to be swayed by an appeal to authority—Rome seemed to carry more weight. Making a very politically correct decision, Oswy, perhaps with tongue in cheek, promptly resolved to take no chances of alienating the doorkeeper of heaven. He decided in favor of Rome, saying he wanted to make sure Peter would welcome him when he came to the gates of the kingdom.

The churches of Northumbria officially accepted the king's decree although there were centers where the Celtic way continued to be observed. Bishop Colman left Lindisfarne and retired with a few of his followers to the old Celtic mission at Iona. Immediately after the decision, a plague swept over Britain killing all the English bishops except one. With the slate wiped clean, five years later, Theodore of Tarsus, a newly appointed and more flexible Archbishop of Canterbury, allowed some Celtic practices to continue. Local customs were respected and compromises were allowed. Although the decision marked the beginning of the end of the Celtic way, traces survived for more than 500 years.

By 630 Rome's authority had been accepted in the southern part of Ireland. After Whitby, northern Ireland and then Scotland followed. Wales resisted until much later. Eventually the two streams of missionary effort blended, giving unity and order from the Roman side and missionary zeal and love of learning from the Celtic. Although differences continued, it took Henry VIII to separate the majority of churches in Great Britain from Roman authority.

Closing Reflection: The Way Not Taken

The abbey Hilda established in the Celtic tradition at Whitby was an exciting and creative witness to its world for more than 200 years until the Danish destroyed it. However, history remembers it as the place where, in matters of doctrine and discipline, the Celtic way began to wane and the Roman way ascend.

Wilfred used the argument in convincing the king at Whitby that authority flowed from Jesus through Peter to the head of the church at Rome. "This passage continues to be one of the storm-centers of New Testament interpretation.... The Roman Catholic Church argues that Peter became the bishop of Rome, and that his power descended through all the bishops of Rome to the Pope, who is the head of the Church and the bishop of Rome."[1]

In Matthew 16:13–20 we find Jesus playing with words: *Peter/ Petros* and *rock/ Petra*. As soon as Peter confesses Jesus is the Messiah, Jesus tells him: you are *Petros*, and on this *Petra* I will build my church. "It is as if Jesus said to Peter, 'Rocky, you are the first person to grasp who I am; you are the first stone in the church I am building.'"[2] Jesus is the real foundation of the church and Peter is the first stone to be built on that foundation.

Jesus also holds the keys to the kingdom (see Revelation 1:8; 3:7), and when Jesus gives Peter "the keys," we understand it is some kind of special transfer of power. To explain what that power is we turn to a reference in Isaiah (22:22) describing Eliakim as the one who has the key to the house of David and only he can open and shut it. As long as he lived he was the faithful steward of the house opening the door in the morning, allowing visitors in, and closing it in the evening. Peter is to be the steward of the kingdom, opening the doors to let thousands come in.

The emphasis in Peter's ministry was on opening, not shutting, doors (Acts 2:41). Peter opened the door to God for thousands of people in the days to come. "The plain fact is that it is not only Peter who has the keys of the kingdom; every Christian has."[3] We are all called to open the door to others so that they may enter into the kingdom.

The ways we take today as Christians are too important and too varied to be dictated either by the state or by one person. Separation of church and state originally protected the church from the state and now protects the state from the church. The way dictated at Whitby combined the power of the state and the power of position to proscribe a particular way of practice.

The way not taken was formed by worshiping, praying, studying, and serving local communities who associated together for a more effective ministry and mission. Its people met for worship at the foot of high crosses, in clearings in the woods, or in simple meeting houses. They were a pilgrim people, ever on the move, always looking ahead. It may well be that the interest in our Celtic heritage is a call to renew this way for today's Christians.

Although the Celtic way became "the way not taken," the way of Ninian, Columba, and Aidan is still with us. The roots of Celtic Christianity are the base from which will spring the way yet to be taken. Inspired by the Holy Spirit, the people of God are beginning to return to a more relational and loving way.

Faith Sharing: The Way

"Do not let your hearts be troubled. Believe in God, believe also in me. In my Father's house there are many dwelling places. If it were not so, would I have told you that I go to prepare a place for you? And if I go and prepare a place for you, I will come again and will take you to myself, so that where I am, there you may be also. And you know the way to the place where I am going." Thomas said to him, "Lord, we do not know where you are going. How can we know the way?"

Jesus said to him, "I am the way, and the truth, and the life. No one comes to the Father except through me. If you know me, you will know my Father also. From now on you do know him and have seen him.

"Believe me that I am in the Father and the Father is in me; but if you do not, then believe me because of the works themselves. Very truly, I tell you, the one who believes in me will also do the works that I do and, in fact, will do greater works than these, because I am going to the Father." (John 14:1–7, 11–12)

Jesus tells Peter, "You cannot go where I am going." To which Peter replies "Lord, where are you going?" Behind Peter's question lies the concern "Why must you go?" Jesus, realizing how Peter is feeling, assures his disciples that he will only be separated from them for a limited time while he goes to make room for them in his Father's house. When he does, he will return for them, and they will join him there forever. The question seems answered yet the dialog goes on. Thomas wonders "How can we know the way?" Then Jesus tells him "I am the way," meaning that we need to trust him to lead us to God. The movement was soon called "The Way" for whatever ways we take, Jesus is ultimately the Way to God.

Personal Reflection

1. How would you respond to someone who tells you: a) "there are many ways to God?" b) "we have the only way to God?"

2. What are some ways that Christians differ on doctrine but work
   together?

Closing Prayer

The love of God flowing free;
The love of God flow out through me.
The peace of God flowing free;
The peace of God flow out through me.
The life of God flowing free;
The life of God flow out through me.[4]

The hill, though high, I covet to ascend,
The difficulty will not me offend;
For I perceive the way to life lies here.
Come, pluck up heart, let us neither faint nor fear;
Better, though difficult, the right way to go,
Than wrong, though easy, where the end is woe.

How do we as Christians—whether mainline or sideline, liberal or conservative, connectional or free—find a community that forms and sustains us in an authentic faith and move out bearing that faith into the structures of our ambiguous society? How do we pass on those forms of community to the next generation?

Loren Mead[1]

PART THREE

Relevance

As pilgrims we have traveled together along the Celtic way from Whithorn to Whitby. If these pages have made a difference in your life, drawn you closer to God, then it will have been a true pilgrimage. The holy sites really are thin places where you may feel close to God and to the holy people who once lived there. Perhaps someday you may experience the feeling as you visit some of these sites in person.

The saints developed rules for living that helped them on their spiritual journey. Now that we have walked with them, they ask us, just as they asked their disciples, to use what they learned in making a difference in the lives of others by loving God, loving people, and witnessing to the way.

In this closing chapter you will read about Bede, the historian, and Cuthbert, the monk. They continue the Lindisfarne tradition, linking it to Durham and to Durham Cathedral, that massive sanctuary in the north that stands as a witness to the faith. It is here each year pilgrims wrestle in a conference with the issues of the Celtic way. You may wish to join them.

Is this way an influence that flows like a stream, sometimes surfacing and flowing freely, and at other times quietly flowing underground nourishing the roots of our faith? We would like to think it is. Loren Mead of the Alban Institute predicts a new role is emerging for us and the churches to which we belong. In the period following the Great Commission, local Christian congregations living in a pagan, and therefore hostile, environment began to organize to do ministry and mission. Their mission surrounded them for it was next door and down the street. Congregations formed associations, supporting and encouraging each other.

When Constantine set the Roman Empire's stamp of approval on Christianity, the old way began to shift. It was assumed your neighbor was now a Christian so the focus of mission shifted to lands afar for there was now no need to witness to those next door. The sacred and secular merged into a cultural religion in which church and state converged. In the drive for unity there was no room for differences, so the church succumbed to standardization. Laity were expected to be loyal to the church in which they were born and to let the clergy worry about theology or mission. Because the post-empire age resembled the pre-empire age in many ways, ministry and mission were done in circumstances similar to those experienced by the Celtic Christians.

This closing chapter summarizes the major characteristics of the Celtic form of Christianity and then introduces some of the ways we can do ministry and mission in the next millennium. Ministry and mission in the twenty-first century: what will it be like? Let's go exploring!

14

Continuing the Quest

I run toward the goal, so that I can win the prize of being called to heaven.

Philippians 3:14

PILGRIM TRAVELS

July 29 to August 2.
Durham

Monday, July 29. A conference on "Celtic Spirituality and Modern Mission" at Durham where I lived and studied in 1984 brings my pilgrim travels to a close. The week begins with morning lectures after which there is a tour of the cathedral. We are meeting in the castle where many of the participants are staying. The quarters are spartan but the food and service are superb and the setting in the ancient dining hall is magnificent!

Tuesday, July 30. The day includes a brief visit to Bede's World, a modern museum that attempts to bring to life the story of early medieval Northumbria through the life and times of the Venerable Bede, one of the great scholars of the early Middle Ages.

Wednesday, July 31. We visit the cathedral library in the afternoon. Unlike the experience at Trinity where we were herded by the Book of Kells, here we are allowed to take several, ancient, illustrated seventh- to twelfth-century manuscripts from the vault to examine. It is exciting to translate the Latin and to consider the time and talent that went into making these brilliantly colored, radiant illustrations.

Thursday, August 1. We view archaeological slides of Northumbrian sites in the morning, including Lindisfarne, Hartlepool, and Whitby. A tour by boat in the afternoon along the river Wear which winds its way around the castle provides the opportunity for some stunning photographs of the massive Norman cathedral which dominates the hill.

Friday, August 2. The Bishop of Durham's Palace, north of the city, is our first stop. Its stained glass windows depict the coming of Christianity to Britain via the Celtic tradition.

Then we paid a visit to a delightful little church in Escomb dating from Anglo-Saxon times. Latin letters are carved in some of the stones indicating they were recycled from Roman fortifications, possibly Hadrian's Wall, to build the church. The wall surrounding the church yard is circular in the ancient Celtic tradition—no corners where evil spirits can hide.

The conference ends in the ancient castle chapel with a worship service patterned after the communion services at Iona. It feels right that my pilgrimage should begin and end with Iona, a contemporary expression of the Celtic way.

Cuthbert (c. 634-687)

After being consecrated at York on Easter, March 26, 685, Cuthbert, the sixth bishop to succeed Aidan at Lindisfarne, spent two years trying to bring a sense of unity within the church in Northumbria. He was probably born of Anglo-Saxon parents in southern Scotland where he grew up working as a shepherd. At age seventeen he entered the Celtic monastery at Melrose. His first major assignment was helping Eata establish a monastery at Ripon. When the king insisted on the Roman rite, the Celtic monks left to be followed by Wilfred, who you will remember was on the other side at Whitby.

In 661 Cuthbert became prior of Melrose where he circulated among the surrounding community, often for weeks at a time, proclaiming God's love. When Colman retired from Lindisfarne to Iona after Whitby, Cuthbert became the prior of Lindisfarne where he reluctantly led his monks to adopt Roman authority and customs. While there, he occasionally retreated to a hermit's solitary life on an island near Lindisfarne. When he retired as prior in 676, he withdrew to the Inner Farne island where Aidan went to observe Lent. There he built an old-style beehive hut of earth and stone for himself and a guest house for visitors. Nine years later he was called to return to Lindisfarne as bishop. A charming and able man, he was known for his preaching, teaching, and pastoral visiting. He died at his hermitage on Inner Farne on March 20, 687, and was buried at Lindisfarne.

On June 7, 793, Viking invaders burned the village and killed many of the monks. The community rebuilt but lived in continual fear of attack until finally, in 875, they left carrying with them the body of Cuthbert, some of Aidan's bones, and the Lindisfarne Gospels. They wandered around northern England carrying his body and relics, until 120 years later at Durham a safe home was found for them. Eventually a cathedral was built on the spot and when Cuthbert's body was placed in it, observers confirmed that it had not deteriorated. Other relics, including a pectoral cross, are in a museum. Cuthbert is buried behind the high altar in Durham Cathedral, sharing with Bede a place of honor and pilgrimage. It seems fitting that the Farne Islands where he spent long periods are now a National Trust sanctuary for birds, seals, and other wildlife.

The Venerable Bede (673-735)

Bede, a monk at the Wearmouth and Jarrow monasteries, is England's first church historian. In 731 at age fifty-nine, he finished his classic work, *The Ecclesiastical History of the English People*. His autobiographical notes at the close of this book indicate that he was born near the newly formed Wearmouth monastery which he joined seven years later. He spent the rest of his life there in the "study of the Scriptures," where it was his "delight to learn or to teach or to write." In 680 a sister monastery was founded at Jarrow. At thirty he became a priest, ordained by John of Beverly who had been trained by Hilda of Whitby.

Bede relied on ancient documents, tradition, accounts from well-traveled scholars, and his own knowledge to compile the history. His stories include the tale of one of King Edwin's aides who likened our life on earth to the swift flight of a sparrow through the hall, from door to door, leaving and returning to the dark winter outside. "Our life appears for a short space, but of what went before or what is to follow, we are utterly ignorant." The Christian faith supplied the answer to this conundrum, leading to the conversion of the English.

Bede's modesty and humility are revealed in his writings—more than twenty-five commentaries on Scripture, a biography of Cuthbert, and a *History of the Abbots of Wearmouth and Jarrow* (c. 730). His life was uneventful for, unlike many of the wandering saints, he traveled little. Two places he visited, Lindisfarne for research and York for study, were relatively short distances away. He preferred monastic duties and writing to consorting with kings and courts. His last days were spent singing psalms and dictating a translation of John into Old English.

Bede died on May 25, 735 and was finally buried in the Galilee chapel in the Durham Cathedral. Often the adjective "venerable," meaning worthy of honor, is associated with his name. A new museum, Bede's World, seeks to preserve the Jarrow site as a center honoring his life, times, and works.

Durham or Dunholm Cathedral

"Grey Towers of Durham, Yet well I love thy mixed and massive piles, Half church of God, half castle 'gainst the Scot." (Sir Walter Scott)

The Christian community at Durham or Dunholm, meaning "hill island," was an extension of Lindisfarne and its monks who wandered around northeastern England in search of a home. Finally, in 995, they discovered a rocky piece of ground almost entirely surrounded by the River Wear that would give them a sense of security. Unlike many monasteries, a bishop rather than an abbot governed the community. The little wooden White Church, erected shortly after their arrival, soon was replaced by one of stone around which people clustered, soon forming a town.

With the Norman conquest in 1066 came changes, including a new and stricter order of Benedictine monks. Since the site was so close to Scotland, the king commissioned the bishop to construct a castle in 1072 to resist any invasion attempts. The Prince Bishops of Durham were empowered with the right to an army, a mint, and a parliament; theirs was a kingdom within a kingdom; church and state merged.

A new bishop had great plans for Durham. In 1093 a massive Norman cathedral was erected high above the bend in the river, dedicated to Cuthbert and built to survive forever. Experienced masons and carpenters were hired in Normandy to create this magnificent Romanesque cathedral.

The following years were not kind to the cathedral. In 1416 after a period of neglect, John Washington, who was an ancestor of George Washington, was appointed prior and began an extensive repair of the cathedral. In September 1650 Cromwell placed 4,000 Scottish prisoners in it. They proceeded to burn anything made of wood to keep warm. In 1832 the University of Durham was established and in 1837 the bishop gave the castle next to the cathedral to the university. The beautiful contemporary stained glass window, "Our Daily Bread," which views the Last Supper from above, was added in 1984. Today the massive cathedral, a World Heritage site, stands high above the city of Durham, a beacon to the pilgrim and a light to the world.

Celtic Christianity: A Summary

The Celtic way includes distinctive characteristics that survive to this day. We see glimpses of these characteristics in the lives of the various holy people of Celtic Christian history:

1. *Disciplines of the desert* (Ninian). The Celtic way values solitude and silence. We are drawn to create times to be alone with God.

2. *Trinity* (Pelagius). The Celtic way is marked by a sense of intimate closeness with the Trinitarian God: Creator, Christ, and Spirit. Conversational prayer is spoken. Jesus is a friend with whom we share the concerns and blessings of everyday life.

3. *A passion for mission* (Patrick). One mission center would spawn another like a spider plant. The Christian faith is spread today by small cells planting new churches or missions.

4. *Soul friend* (Brigid). The Celts sought a "soul friend," a spiritual guide or personal mentor with whom they could "share the significant and often insignificant experiences of their lives. Often in the telling, they would discover that the seemingly insignificant events are really the most important of all, the times when and places where God speaks."[1] Our soul friends are those who listen to our experiences and help us discover how God is touching our lives.

5. *Nature* (David). It is God's world and it is good. We both fear and respect the environment and the animals and plants that inhabit it. There is a sense of comfort and security that God will be with us through the storms of life no matter happens.

6. *Thin places* (Ciaran). Time for those with a Celtic nature is fluid rather than rigid. Thin places are sites where one experiences a very thin boundary between this world and the next.

7. *Exploration* (Kevin's scribal scholars). Many Celtic Christians experienced the "white martyrdom" of living far from home and family because they were called to go wherever the need existed to make disciples. Many people today have this same deep desire to go where there is a need for their service.

8. *Community* (Columba). The mission centers or monasteries were actually small villages. Each center adopted its own rules for living together. Our communities (congregations) nurture and sustain our faith. We care for our friends with whom we work, worship, and play.

9. *Ordinary life* (Aidan). God is found, not only at the end of time, but also where the kingdom is being lived by God's people today. Ordinary events are exciting, not boring. Our daily routines and yearly observances are regular reminders of the closeness of God.

10. *Tales told* (Hilda). Relationships are rooted in the sharing of our stories, our music, our dance, and our literature. Often this happens in small groups. Our story encourages others to live in a closer relationship with God.

11. *Love of learning* (Bede and Durham). A love of learning springs from Celtic roots. Monastic schools flourished with pilgrim scholars coming from all over Europe. The Celtic way surfaces today in those who have a love of learning, especially of the Scriptures.

12. *Place* (Pilgrimage). Pilgrimage, becoming all one can be through contact with the holy, is important. We travel to the thin places where God seems closer. As we combine the outward journey with the inner journey of the soul, we connect with God and our lives are transformed.

Closing Reflection:
Celtic Roots in Millennium Missions

We have arrived at the end of our journey together. The pilgrim path to Christian maturity moves through the stages of being a pagan to becoming a believer to discovering discipleship and finally finding a mission or ministry. Mature Christians, driven by their faith, desire to continually learn from Jesus and are actively involved in a mission. As missionaries, we are doing what Jesus commissions us to do, to witness to the world and make disciples.

The Celtic Christians did mission in a pagan, pre-Christian age much like the one we are rapidly entering. We can no longer assume that everyone is a Christian. We can no longer assume people will support Christian values. We can no longer assume the church will have a special place in the life of our secular communities. We can no longer assume mission is only in a distant land; it is just outside of our door. Right around the corner are some of the richest mission fields in our world. For example, more than fifty percent of the people in the United States are unchurched.

As missionaries, how do we reach the coming generations with the gospel? The best way is to share the story of what the gospel has meant to us in our lives, with our friends, family, and acquaintances and then invite them to be part of the people who are on the pilgrimage with us. When and if they respond to our invitation to worship with us, they may be beginning a spiritual journey that will last forever.

We cannot long minister in a pagan world with all the stress that may occur in so doing without some way of renewing our spiritual life, of recharging our batteries. What may we do? Here are a few specific suggestions.

1. *Personal spiritual journey.* Continue your journey with a caring circle, cluster, or small group possibly formed around the study of the Bible. Most of us need to belong to a caring circle of friends that will encourage our faith, help us cope, pray with and for us, listen to our story, and treat what we say with respect. Such groups, writes Tex Sample, give us "the power to 'hunker down' and 'make it through the night.'"[2]

2. *Effective ministry.* If you are not an active member in a congregation, become one. You may have rejected the institutional church in the past for its many failings—having been a pastor for more than twenty-five years, I know what many of them are. The church is changing and you are called to be part of that changing ministry and mission. New forms are being created in response to the continually changing world in which we exist. Find them or create them. We are called, as were the Celtic Christians, to reinvent the church as we go. The early Celtic missionaries were respectful of the traditions of others and tried, when appropriate, to incorporate them into what they were doing. We need to risk change and do the same.

Effective ministry will emphasize showing God cares and so do we by healing those who are hurting, sharing our stories of our walk with Jesus, and supporting others on the journey by meeting their personal and spiritual needs. Respect for clergy and church leaders will be based on developing these relationships rather than on traditional respect for the office, which has eroded.

Effective ministry will include inspirational preaching anchored solidly in the Scriptures. In many congregations this will include using the ecumenical lectionary. These great texts of the Bible are made even more meaningful by studying them together in small groups earlier in the week. The ministry of teaching nurtures faith, models the life of prayer, relates the Bible to daily life, and trains laity for ministry and mission.

3. *Integrity.* The congregation is a mission center, welcoming believers, training disciples, and sending apostles or missionaries. We have said we care; integrity is showing that we do by helping others connect with God. There is a shift going on right now from surrogate mission (someone else doing it), to a local, hands-on mission (members doing it). Since that is true, all members of the congregation will need to be trained to do ministry and mission, with both clergy and experienced pastoral leaders called upon to train them. You are invited to become involved.

4. *Support.* Because the mission field now surrounds the local congregation, regional and national church organizations must make the encouragment of vital congregations a priority. They have always focused on missions; now they need to reverse the emphasis on helping missions in distant lands to enabling the local congregations, the missions in their own regions, to survive and thrive. As they do, relationships will be renewed and associations strengthened.

5. *Purpose.* We need to have a vision that enables us to make sense of the pieces of our lives. Our congregations should also seek to summarize their mission and the passions of their people in a short, simple statement that could be used frequently and posted as a reminder. Here is the vision of one church, the Church of the Brethren: "Continuing the work of Jesus. Peacefully. Simply. Together."

Congregations are about helping us on the journey of becoming believers, then disciples and finally missionaries, for the goal of the church is simply lives changed for Jesus. Does that sound familiar? Of course it does. You have just finished reading about a people who had that goal. Perhaps we can learn from them.

Conclusion

Ian Bradley concludes his excellent book, *The Celtic Way*, with these observations

> The Celtic Church...was not a highly organized and hierarchical institution but rather a loose grouping of local communities of prayer, learning and hospitality....Its members met for worship...at the foot of high crosses, in forest glades and clearings or in simple wattle and daub huts. They were a pilgrim people, ever on the move and always looking ahead. It may well be that this is the way forward now for Christians in the so-called developed world and that the third millennium will see a return to those localized and provisional communities which flourished in the first one....
>
> The Celtic monasteries were not just mission stations—they were centers of culture and enlightenment, little colonies of heaven which witnessed not just to the narrow Gospel or individual redemption but to Jesus' wider promise of life in all its fulness....
>
> If the churches are to make any kind of effective stand for the Christian values which are increasingly under attack it is surely by following the example of the Celtic monasteries and becoming little pools of gentleness and enlightenment, oases of compassion and charity in the ever extending desert of secular materialism.[3]

Celtic Christianity continues to inspire through the tales that are told of the lives that lived it. May it come alive in our lives and churches and world.

Faith Sharing:
Pressing on Toward the Goal

Not that I have already obtained this or have already reached the goal; but I press on to make it my own, because Christ Jesus has made me his own. Beloved, I do not consider that I have made it my own; but this one thing I do: forgetting what lies behind and straining forward to what lies ahead, I press on toward the goal for the prize of the heavenly call of God in Christ Jesus. Let those of us then who are mature be of the same mind; and if you think differently about anything, this too God will reveal to you. Only let us hold fast to what we have attained.

Brothers and sisters, join in imitating me, and observe those who live according to the example you have in us. For many live as enemies of the cross of Christ; I have often told you of them, and now I tell you even with tears. Their end is destruction; their god is the belly; and their glory is in their shame; their minds are set on earthly things. But our citizenship is in heaven, and it is from there that we are expecting a Savior, the Lord Jesus Christ. He will transform the body of our humiliation that it may be conformed to the body of his glory, by the power that also enables him to make all things subject to himself. Therefore, my brothers and sisters, whom I love and long for, my joy and crown, stand firm in the Lord in this way, my beloved. (Philippians 3:12—4:1)

What is life like? It is like running a race. We run until we cross the finish line and complete the journey. Then, unlike the usual race, a prize is given to everyone who finishes. The more our faith deepens, the more we learn about Jesus, and the more we are involved in ministry, the nearer we come to the goal. We follow Paul's example and that of others who, like him, follow the way of Jesus. If we also teach by word and example, we must realize we must be careful about our conduct so that others will not stumble and fall because of it. As believers, we are citizens of heaven. Finally Paul encourages us to be faithful, and then he concludes with an expression of his joy and pride in his friends.

Personal Reflection

1. To what mission or ministry is God calling you? Spend some time over the next few weeks trying to discern whether you are where God wants you to be right now, or whether it may be time to begin something new.
2. Which one of the Celtic saints, holy people, would you like as a soul friend, one to advise you on how to run the race? Why?

Closing Prayer

God before us,
God behind us,
God above us,
God beneath us,
God beside us,
God within us,
May God bless us
on our journey. Amen.

ENDNOTES

PART ONE: CELTIC ROOTS

1. Diane J. Shearer. Unpublished poem. Used by permission.

2. Thomas Naylor, William Willimon, and Magdalena Naylor, *The Search for Meaning* (Nashville: Abingdon Press, 1994). Used by permission.

Chapter Two: The Celts

1. Julius Caesar, *The Gallic Wars*, translated by John Warrington (Norwalk, Connecticut: The Heritage Press, 1983), p. 3.

2. Gerhard Herm, *The Celts: The People who Came out of the Darkness* (New York: St. Martin's Press, 1977), p. 46-47.

3. David Adam, *Border Lands* (London: SPCK, 1994), p. 5. © David Adam, 1991. Reprinted by permission of SPCK.

Chapter Three: The Romans

1. G. R. D. McLean, *Poems of the Western Highlanders* (London: SPCK, 1961), quoted in David Adam, *Border Lands* (London: SPCK, 1994), p. 55. Used by permission.

PART TWO: RELATIONSHIPS: SAINTS AND SITES

1. M. Scott Peck, *In Search of Stones* (New York: Hyperion, 1995), p. 222. Used by permission. © M. Scott Peck.

Chapter Four: Ninian

1. Henri J. M. Nouwen, *The Way of the Heart: Desert Spirituality and Contemporary Ministry* (New York: Harper Collins, 1981), p. 49. © 1981 by Henri J. M. Nouwen.

Chapter Five: Pelagius

1. George Markstein and David Tomblin, "1. Arrival" from *The Prisoner*. The Prisoner Television Series. An ITC production by Everyman Films Limited in 1966/67.

Chapter Six: Patrick

1. Saint Patrick's *Confession*, translated by Ludwig Bieler. As found in Saint Patrick's Trian Visitor Complex, Armagh, Northern Ireland BT61 7BA.

2. Peter Harbison and Jacqueline O'Brien, *Ancient Ireland: From Prehistory to the Middle Ages* (New York: Oxford University Press, 1996), p. 46. Used by permission.

3. Lyle Schaller, *21 Bridges to the 21st Century: The Future of Pastoral Ministry* (Nashville: Abingdon Press, 1994), p. 150. Used by permission.

4. N. D. O'Donoghue, "St. Patrick's Breastplate" in *An Introduction to Celtic Christianity*, ed. James P. Mackey (Edinburgh: T&T Clark, 1995), p. 46.

Chapter Seven: Brigid of Kildare

1. Taken from page 73 of *The Celtic Way* by Ian Bradley published and copyright 1993 by Darton, Longman & Todd Ltd. and used by permission of the publishers.

2. Brian Brendan O'Malley, *A Pilgrim's Manual: St. Davids* (Marlborough, England: Paulinus Press, 1985), p. 138. Used with permission.

3. Robert Van de Weyer, *Celtic Fire: The Passionate Religious Vision of Ancient Britain and Ireland* (New York: Doubleday, 1990), p.39-40. Used by permission.

Chapter Eight: David

1. Nona Rees, *The Misericords of St. Davids* (St. Davids: RJL Smith, 1995), p. 12. Used by permission.

2. O'Malley, *A Pilgrim's Manual*, p. 26. Used with permission.

Chapter Nine: Ciaran of Clonmacnoise

1. Adam, *Border Lands*, p. 200. Used by permission.

Chapter Ten: Kevin of Glendalough

1. Thomas Cahill, *How the Irish Saved Civilization* (New York: Doubleday, 1995). Used by permission.

Chapter Twelve: Aidan and Lindisfarne

1. Esther de Waal, *Every Earthly Blessing* (Ann Arbor: Servant Publications, 1991), p. 20, 21. Used by permission of the author.

2. John Coburn, *Prayer and Personal Religion* (Philadelphia: Westminster, 1957), p. 49. Used by permission.

3. David Adam, *Border Lands*, p. 23. Used by permission.

Chapter Thirteen: Hilda of Whitby

1. William Barclay, *The Daily Study Bible: The Gospel of Matthew, vol. 2* (Edinburgh: Saint Andrew Press, 1958; reprint Philadelphia: Westminster Press), p.153ff. Permission granted by Westminster Press.

2. Barclay, ibid.

3. Barclay, ibid.

4. Adam, *Border Lands*, p. 50. Used by permission.

PART THREE: RELEVANCE: MINISTRY AND MISSION

1. Loren Mead, *The Once and Future Church: Reinventing the Congregation for a New Mission Frontier* (Washington: Alban Institute, 1991), p. 92. Reprinted with permission from Alban Institute, Inc., 7315 Wisconsin Ave., Suite 1250W, Bethesda, Maryland 20814-3211. All rights reserved.

Chapter Fourteen: Continuing the Quest

1. Excerpted from *Wisdom of the Celtic Saints* by Edward C. Sellner, p. 27. Copyright 1993 by Ave Maria Press, Notre Dame, IN 46556. Used with permission of the publisher.

2. Tex Sample, *Ministry in an Oral Culture: Living with Will Rogers, Uncle Remus, and Minnie Pearl* (Louisville: Westminster/John Knox Press, 1994), p. 23. Used by permission.

3. Bradley, *The Celtic Way*, p.118-119. Used by permission.

TALES WE TELL ALONG THE WAY

Suggestions for Small Group Study

Pilgrimages are often best taken with friends, so invite your friends to read this book and discuss it with you around the kitchen table; or organize a study group in your home, church, school, or place of work and share your stories with each other. Take a pilgrimage together.

My experience has been that if you have a morning group it is best to start with something to drink, often coffee or juice, and something light to eat, such as cookies. Evening groups often work best when refreshments are served afterwards. Whatever time of day or schedule you choose, make this a fun and welcoming time.

The prayer at the end of each chapter can be an effective way to close, especially in the form of a unison prayer. You may also wish to start with a prayer circle by standing, joining hands, and having each person mention one or two things briefly in prayer.

You may find help for planning a study of the selected Scripture text in each chapter from the Serendipity Bible which is specifically written for small group study. I used LESSONmaker 4 for Windows, a computer program developed by NavPress Software (1934 Rutland Drive, Suite 500, Austin, Texas 78758) to create the outlines for the small group sessions I led with my congregation.

GUIDEBOOKS FOR THE PILGRIM

A Selected Bibliography

PART ONE
Celtic Roots

1. Chadwick, Nora, *The Celts*. Pelican Books, 1971; reprint ed. London: Penguin Books Ltd., 1991. The classic on the Celts.

2. Nouwen, Henri J. M., *The Way of the Heart: Desert Spirituality and Contemporary Ministry*. New York: Harper Collins Publishers, 1981.

PART TWO
Relationships: Soul Friends and Thin Places

1. Adam, David, *Border Lands: The Best of David Adam*. London: SPCK, 1994. Prayers in the Celtic tradition. A must for your Celtic library.

2. Bradley, Ian, *The Celtic Way*. London: Darton, Longman and Todd, Ltd., 1993. The best overview of Celtic Christianity.

3. Delap, Dana, *Celtic Saints*. Andover, England: Pitkin Pictorials, 1995. An excellent summary in twenty colorful pages by the Northumbrian Community.

4. De Waal, Esther, *The Celtic Way of Prayer: The Recovery of the Religious Imagination*. New York: Doubleday, 1997.

5. _____*The Celtic Vision*. London: Darton, Longman and Todd, Ltd, 1988; reprint edition, Petersham, Massachusetts: St. Bede's Publications, 1988. A basic book.
Selections from the *Carmina Gadelica* by Alexander Carmichael.

6. Ferguson, John, *Pelagius: A Historical and Theological Study*. W. Heffer & Sons, Ltd., 1956. Dissertation for the University of Cambridge.

7. Harbison, Peter and O'Brien, Jacqueline, *Ancient Ireland: From Prehistory to the Middle Ages*. New York: Oxford University Press, 1996. Photographs by Jacqueline O'Brien. A lavishly illustrated and well-written coffeetable book, well worth the price.

8. Harbison, Peter, *Irish High Crosses*. Drogheda, Ireland: Boyne Valley Honey Company, 1994. A detailed pocket size guidebook to the high crosses.

9. Joyce, Timothy, *Celtic Christianity: A Sacred Tradition, A Vision of Hope*. Maryknoll, NY: Orbis Books, 1998. An Irish view of Celtic spirituality by a Benedictine monk.

10. Mackey, James P., editor. *An Introduction to Celtic Christianity*. Edinburgh: T&T Clark, 1995. An excellent scholarly anthology on Celtic Christianity. See especially *Celtic Theology: Pelagius* by M. Forthomme Nicholson.

11. Marshall, David, *Pilgrim Ways: A Holiday Guide to the Christian "Holy Places" of Britain and Ireland*. Grantham, England: Autumn House, 1993. Traveling for fun.

12. Pennick, Nigel, *Celtic Sacred Landscapes*. New York: Thames and Hudson, 1996. This is a beautifully designed book with a gazetteer of notable Celtic sacred places.

13. Raine, Andy and Skinner, John T. *Celtic Daily Prayer: A Northumbrian Office*. London: Marshall Pickering, 1994.

14. The Northumbrian Community, *Celtic Night Prayer*. London, Marshall Pickering, 1996. This and *Celtic Daily Prayer* are a mix of daily readings and prayers. Both are very popular books.

15. Sellner, Edward, *Wisdom of the Celtic Saints*. Notre Dame, Indiana: Ave Maria Press, 1993. Well-done retelling of the stories and sayings of the Celtic saints. The line drawing illustrations by Susan McLean-Keeney are superb.

16. Sheldrake, Philip, *Living Between Worlds: Place and Journey in Celtic Spirituality*. Boston: Cowley Publications, 1995. See the chapter on "Iona: Place and Pilgrimage."

17. Toulson, Shirley, *Celtic Journeys in Scotland and the North of England*. London: Fount Paperbacks, Harper Collins Publishers, 1995. For the traveler to Whithorn, Iona, Lindisfarne, and Durham among other places.

18. Van de Weyer, Robert, editor, *Celtic Fire: The Passionate Religious Vision of Ancient Britain and Ireland*. New York: Doubleday, 1990. The chapter, "A Celtic Pilgrimage," inspired my study leave circle tour of Celtic sites.

PART THREE

Relevance: Ministry and Mission Today

1. Bede. *The Ecclesiastical History of the English People*. New York: Oxford University, 1994.

2. Callahan, Kennon. *Effective Church Leadership: Building on the Twelve Keys.* San Francisco: Jossey-Bass Publishers.

2. Mead, Loren, *The Once and Future Church: Reinventing the Congregation for a New Mission Frontier.* Washington: Alban Institute, 1991.

3. Sample, Tex. *Ministry in an Oral Culture: Living with Will Rogers, Uncle Remus, and Minnie Pearl.* Louisville, Kentucky: Westminster/John Knox Press, 1994. A humorous but serious attempt to analyze oral communication today.

4. Schaller, Lyle, *21 Bridges to the 21st Century: The Future of Pastoral Ministry.* Nashville: Abingdon Press, 1994.

5. Shaw, Martin, *Island Soldiers: The History of the Celtic Saints* (video). Newbridge Communications, 1997. Views of many of the sites mentioned in this book. Call 800/257-5126 to order.

PLACES ALONG THE WAY

Inns, Rooms, and Board

I traveled alone staying often in bed and breakfasts and small hotels. The accommodations varied.

1. *Oban*. Mrs. Kirsteen Clark, 5 High Street, Oban, Argyll PA34 4BG. Phone 01631 562475.

2. *Iona*. Mrs. Gilbert Black, Plachan Corrach, Isle of Iona, Argyll, PA76 6SP. Phone: 1681-700323. A small working farm. Delicious meals.

3. *Iona*. Duncraig, Isle of Iona, Argyll PA76 6SP. Phone: 01681 700202. Christian Quiet House. Iona Cornerstone Foundation Ltd.

4. *Whithorn*. George and Ann Stables; Corsbie Road, Newton Stewart DG8 6YB. Phone 1671-402157. They served a delicious meal even when I arrived at a late hour.

5. *Lindisfarne*. Marygate/Cambridge House, Holy Island, Berwick upon Tweed, Northumberland TD15 2SD. Phone 1289 389246. A Christian retreat center.

6. *Whitby*. The Sea Brink Hotel, 3 Beach Street, Filey, North Yorkshire YO14 9LA. Phone 1723-513257. Small hotel with magnificent views of the bay. Olga Carter, hostess.

7. *Little Gidding*. Society of Christ the Sower, Little Gidding, Huntingdon PE17 5RJ. Phone 1832-293383. My hostess was Margaret Smith. Christian retreat center.

8. *St. Davids*. Mrs. Rona M. Liggitt, Ty Olaf, Mount Gardens, St. Davids, Dyfed Wales SA62 6BS. Phone: 1437-720885. Lovely home. She sings in her church choir.

9. *St. Deiniol's*. Residential Library. Hawarden, Deeside, Clwyd CH5 3DF. Phone 1244 532350. Northern Wales near Chester.

10. *Durham*. Durham Ecumenical Seminars, The Castle - Palace Green, University of Durham, Durham, Northern England. Phone 1913-743865. Two week study course each summer.

11. *Dublin*. Trinity College, Dublin.

Of Related Interest

The Soul of Celtic Spirituality
In the Lives of Its Saints
Michael Mitton

Here, Michael Mitton introduces readers to the Celtic love of wholeness as reflected in its stories, traditions, rituals, and above all in the lives of its saints. Mitton invites readers to study the Celtic Church to rediscover some of the very important "strands of faith" that were clearly evident—and that are just as relevant for Christians today.
ISBN: 0-89622-662-X, 160 pp, 9.95

Celtic Blessings and Prayers
Making All Things Sacred
Brendan O'Malley

Here is a collection of ancient and newly written prayers and rituals. Blessings are given for every area of human life: family, friends, each room of the house, the meal table, work, journeys, rites of passage, the sick, seasons of the year, and much more. No task is too humble nor is any object too lowly to be offered back to God in thanksgiving and praise.
ISBN 0-89622-957-2, 208 pp, $12.95

Towards a History of Irish Spirituality
Peter O'Dwyer, O.Carm.

Examines the development of the Catholic Church starting in early Christian times in Ireland, showing what Irish spirituality means and the thoughts of the people in each period of history.
ISBN: 1-85607-124-3 (order L-13), 288 pp, $17.95

In Search of Columba
Lesley Whiteside

1997 marks the 1400th anniversary of the death of St. Columba. Here is a portrait of both the historical and the spiritual Columba and his contribution to Celtic spirituality. Includes many quotations and anecdotes which help to bring alive this fascinating Celtic figure. (order L-76), 128 pp, $9.95

Available from religious bookstores or:

XXIII TWENTY-THIRD PUBLICATIONS
P.O. Box 180 • Mystic, CT 06355 • 1-800-321-0411
Call for a free catalog